GREAT BEGINNINGS
AND ENDINGS

GREAT

BEGINNINGS

AND

ENDINGS

PENING AND
CLOSING LINES
OF GREAT NOVELS

GEORGIANNE ENSIGN

■ HarperPerennial
A Division of HarperCollins*Publishers*

FIRST EDITION

Library of Congress Cataloging-in-Publication Data

Great beginnings and endings : opening and closing lines of great novels / [compiled by] Georgianne Ensign.
    p.   cm.
First work originally published: Great beginnings. 1st ed. New York, NY : HarperCollins Publishers, © 1993. Second work originally published: Great endings. 1st ed, New York, NY : HarperCollins Publishers, © 1995.
    Includes indexes.
    ISBN 0-06-095192-3
    1. Fiction—Technique. 2. Openings (Rhetoric) 3. Endings (Rhetoric) 4. Quotations, English. I. Ensign, Georgianne. II. Great endings. III. Title.
PN3365.G73   1996
808.3—dc20   96-3525

96 97 98 99 00 ❖/RRD10 9 8 7 6 5 4 3 2 1

To Yester Ensign

Contents ❧

Acknowledgments ❦

This book combines two previously published volumes, *Great Beginnings* and *Great Endings*, although, inevitably, some material from the originals has been cut in the interest of brevity. The result is a collection of little gems that should probably be called *Greatest Beginnings and Endings.*

The idea for the books occurred to me when my agent, Julian Bach, having been handed a manuscript of mine—an Edwardian love story—declared (somewhat jokingly) that the first test he applied to a novel was its beginning sentence. This passing comment made me curious about the beginnings of the classics of literature, and the search rapidly grew into *Great Beginnings*, for which I thank him. *Great Endings* was a natural sequel, a fact confirmed for me by the number of readers who independently suggested that I write it. I hastened to inform each of them that it had been conceived even before the first book was written; still, I would like to thank them all for their votes of confidence.

I am deeply grateful to the staff of the remarkable Kent School John Gray Park Library—where much of the research for these books was conducted—especially Director Marel d'Orbessan Rogers, Judith K. Dike, Lia D. Smits and Leslie S. Snowden; and of the equally surprising Kent Memorial Library and its Head Librarian Deborah Custer, for their enthusiastic help and unfailing confidence.

For their assistance in my research and in extending me permission to publish the wonderful manuscript illustrations in this book, I thank Michael Asquith, Professor Quentin Bell, Joseph Heller, Merlin Holland, and Jill Faulkner Summers; also Patricia C. Willis, Danielle C. McClellan (Beinecke Library, Yale University), Francis O. Mattson (Berg Collection, The New York Public Library), Dr. Charles Cutter (Brandeis University Library), C. M. Hall, Alan Marshall, M. Mohamed (The British Library), Kathryn White (The Brontë Society), R.N.R. Peers and R. M. de Peyer (Dorset County Museum), Leslie A. Morris, Emily C. Walhout (Houghton Library, Harvard University), Jacqueline Cox (King's College Library, Cambridge), Sheila Mortimer (The National Trust), Charles E. Pierce Jr., Inge Dupont, Christine Nelson and Kris Elen MacKenzie (Pierpont Morgan Library), Wayne Furman (Office of Special Collections, New York Public Library), R. Russell Maylone (Northwestern University Library), Dr. William L. Joyce, Margaret M. Sherry, Alice V. Clark, Charles E. Greene and Don C. Skemer (Princeton University Libraries), Una O'Sullivan (Royal Commission on Historical Manuscripts), Anita Goodwin (The Society of Authors), Christine L. Penney (University of Birmingham Library), Gene K. Rinkel and Todd E. Fell (University Library, University of Illinois at Urbana-Champaign), Alice R. Cotten (University of North Carolina at Chapel Hill), Cathy Henderson, Sally Leach, Diane Goldenberg-Hart, Heather Moore and Barbara Smith-LaBorde (University of Texas at Austin), Michael Plunkett, Gregory A. Johnson and Adrienne Cannon (University of Virginia Library), and David C. Devenish (Wisbech and Fenland Museum). Also Alan A. Meyer (Halsey Meyer Higgins), William Heinemann Ltd., Julie Fallowfield (McIntosh and Otis, Inc.), Owen Laster

(William Morris Agency), Craig Tenney and Joanna Rakoff (Harold Ober Associates, Inc.), Fiona Batty (the Peters Fraser & Dunlop Group Ltd.), Gerald J. Pollinger and Margaret Pepper (Laurence Pollinger Ltd.), Agnes Fisher, Edith Golub and Ron Hussey (Simon & Schuster), Linda Shaughnessy and Beth Crockett (A. P. Watt Ltd.), and Paul Gitlin (Estate of Thomas Wolfe).

Personal thanks are also due to Yester Ensign; Robin Hulf; my editor Cynthia Barrett; and my husband, Richard T. Kent.

GREAT BEGINNINGS . . .

1 ❧ INTRODUCTION

I don't know if you have had the same experience, but the snag I always come up against when I'm telling a story is this dashed difficult problem of where to begin it," confides P. G. Wodehouse's winsome dilettante, Bertie Wooster, on the first page of one of the classic Jeeves novels, *Right Ho, Jeeves*. "It's a thing you don't want to go wrong over, because one false step and you're sunk. I mean, if you fool about too long at the start, trying to establish atmosphere, as they call it, and all that sort of rot, you fail to grip and the customers walk out on you."

If Wodehouse shared this problem with his guileless character, which is probable, but still difficult to believe, he knew how to find the solution. *Right Ho, Jeeves* begins with a deceptively simple first line directed to the inimitable gentleman's gentleman that promises Wodehouse cognoscenti hours of sophisticated silliness:

"'Jeeves,' I said, 'may I speak frankly?'"

Every novelist, from the absolute novice to Thomas Hardy, Ernest Hemingway, and Norman Mailer, has known the exciting but intimidating challenge of that first sentence, the imperative to grip a reader's attention sufficiently to carry him on through the only slightly less daunting second sentence into the next paragraph and to the end of the page. Everyone has had to begin somewhere.

Vita Sackville-West began *her* novel, *The Edwardians,* by writing about—how to begin a novel. "Among the many problems which beset the novelist, not the least weighty is the choice of the moment at which to begin his novel," the book opens. "It is necessary, it is indeed unavoidable, that he should intersect the lives of his dramatis personae at a given hour; all that remains is to decide which hour it shall be, and in what situation they shall be discovered." There were not only the life and the death of the character to consider as starting points, but a whole continuum of episodes and circumstances, hours and moments, from which to choose. Any of them might be valid, but the novelist could select only one.

So, where to begin?

Some novelists have strolled unhurriedly into their stories, some leaped directly into the action, some have found a few words sufficient, some an entire page. Some first lines are so remarkable they have become memorable as famous quotations. Surely Herman Melville as he wrote, "Call me Ishmael," or Charles Dickens, as he dipped his pen and began, "It was the best of times, it was the worst of times . . . ," must have smiled with satisfaction. There is little doubt when it is right.

And when it is wrong. For the lack of just the right first line, novels have languished unwritten. And although it is obvious that an opening that proved exactly right for Joseph Conrad or for William Faulkner would not have been possible for Anthony Burgess or John Updike (and even inconceivable that *Lord Jim* could have begun as *Nostromo* does), yet it is illuminating to compare the techniques novelists have used and the choices they have made.

Great Beginnings and Endings is intended to bring the delight of recognition to all readers of novels—whether writers or not—by recalling some of the great beginning and ending sentences of novels that have achieved distinction and reputation. However, if you are a promising novelist wondering how to begin, reading through this collection of opening and closing lines may give you the courage and the inspiration you need, by showing you the simplicity and variety of some of the solutions to the writer's dilemma that others have found. Each excerpt in this section includes just enough to indicate where the beginning is leading, and to show how the author contrived to follow that first, miraculous thought. Excerpts in the second section treat the ending in much same way, with a collection of brilliant codas. For the sake of easy comparison, selections have been grouped into categories that illustrate how authors widely separated by style, culture, and time—even centuries—have relied upon surprisingly similar techniques.

If the excerpts are unsatisfying in any way, it is because they are incomplete; they are not meant to stand alone. In fact, it is an indication of their success that we want to read more of some books we may never have considered taking off a shelf. In this way, *Great Beginnings and Endings* quite naturally forms a solid and varied reading list, encompassing authors from the beginning of the nineteenth century—when the novel as we have come to know it took form under the pens of Jane Austen and Sir Walter Scott—to the present. Although concentrating on English-speaking authors, the book includes the work of novelists writing in other languages when omission would leave serious gaps. How could one ignore, for instance, *Madame Bovary, War and Peace,* or *Buddenbrooks*?

Of course, *Great Beginnings and Endings* makes no claim to be exhaustive, and although an effort has been made to include the great classics of literature, inevitably personal favorites may be missing. It is, however, a great beginning.

2 ❧ ONCE UPON A TIME

he novel is, first of all, the telling of a story. Whether it begins at the beginning with the birth of a hero, at the end with his death, or somewhere in the middle in his youth or his prime as he approaches the event that will differentiate his life from all others, a story must be told. Who is to tell it— the hero or heroine, a casual witness, the author-creator himself, or the author masquerading as another writer—is one of the first choices the novelist must make.

In most cases, the choice is an unconscious one. For although it is perhaps simplistic to say that the story dictates its own teller, the novel probably *does* "come" to the author in one of these voices, just as a story suggests itself to a writer as a novel, rather than a play or a film. And so *Great Expectations* and *The Magus* are narrated by their heroes, *Moby-Dick* and *My Ántonia* are related by witnesses, and *The Portrait of a*

Lady and *Tess of the d'Urbervilles* are told by their authors.

Of course, each of these novels could have been told from another point of view. Witness the recent successful retelling of Stevenson's *Dr. Jekyll and Mr. Hyde* through the eyes of the housemaid instead of the lawyer, Mr. Utterson. Or the attempted re-creation, by means of a letter from Heathcliff, of the years Heathcliff was mysteriously absent from Wuthering Heights, in the novel *H*. But although other approaches were possible, they would have resulted in very different stories. *Wuthering Heights* might have been much more interesting psychologically if Emily Brontë had chosen to allow Heathcliff to tell his own story. But she knew instinctively that the strange blackness of his personality was far more effectively revealed from the innocent lips of the housekeeper, Nelly Dean, and the tenant, Mr. Lockwood. On the other hand, *Rebecca* told in the words of the second Mrs. de Winter forces us to experience her growing fears in a way that would not be as possible with the intervention of a narrator. Conversely, the vast Russian tapestry of *War and Peace* could never have been woven in such brilliant detail by a girlish Natasha (or even by a Pierre, despite his infatuation with Napoleon); it required the omniscience of the novelist. In each of these novels, the chosen point of view is well-suited to the requirements of the story.

Storytelling through the ages has depended upon these three points of view. Which is the most natural? Is it the story told in the first person by the actor of the drama, with the intimacy of a confession? "As soon as I got to Borstal they made me a long-distance cross-country runner. I suppose they thought I was just the build for it because I was long and skinny for my age (and still am) and in any case I didn't mind it much, to tell you the truth, because running had always been made much of in our family, especially running away from the police" (Alan Sillitoe, *The Loneliness of the Long-Distance Runner*). Is it the story confided by the witness, who shapes the character and the plot by what he chooses to tell and not tell? "I had the story, bit by bit, from various people, and, as generally happens in such cases, each time it was a different story" (Edith Wharton, *Ethan Frome*). Or is it the story told from the omniscient point of view of the author, in the tradition of once-upon-a-time? "There once lived, in a sequestered part of the county of Devonshire, one Mr. Godfrey Nickleby, a worthy gentleman, who, taking it into his head rather late in life that he must get married, and not being young enough or rich enough to aspire to the hand of a lady of fortune, had wedded an old flame out of mere attachment, who in her turn had taken him for the same reason" (Charles Dickens, *Life and Adventures of Nicholas Nickleby*). Each is a totally valid choice, but although it may sound somewhat mysterious, in the end it is usually the story that determines the storyteller.

The selections in this chapter show how novelists have used two of these voices: narration by the main character and narration by a witness. The third, narration by the author, which presents many more options to the writer, is illustrated by most of the chapters that follow in this section.

The First Person in Person ❧
The hero tells the story in his own words.

I was born in 1927, the only child of middle-class parents, both English, and themselves born in the grotesquely elongated shadow, which they never rose sufficiently above history to leave, of that monstrous dwarf Queen Victoria. I was sent to a public school, I wasted two years doing my national service, I went to Oxford; and there I began to discover I was not the person I wanted to be.
> —JOHN FOWLES, *The Magus*

Whether I shall turn out to be the hero of my own life, or whether that station will be held by anybody else, these pages must show. To begin my life with the beginning of my life, I record that I was born (as I have been informed and believe) on a Friday, at twelve o'clock at night. It was remarked that the clock began to strike, and I began to cry, simultaneously.
> —CHARLES DICKENS,
> *The Personal History of David Copperfield*

My wound is geography. It is also my anchorage, my port of call.

I grew up slowly beside the tides and marshes of Colleton; my arms were tawny and strong from working long days on the shrimp boat in the blazing South Carolina heat. Because I was a Wingo, I worked as soon as I could walk; I could pick a blue crab clean when I was five. I had killed my first deer by the age of seven, and at nine was regularly putting meat on my family's table. I was born and raised on a Carolina sea island and I carried the sunshine of the low-country, inked in dark gold, on my back and shoulders.

—PAT CONROY, Prologue, *The Prince of Tides*

Call me Jonah. My parents did, or nearly did. They called me John.

Jonah—John—if I had been a Sam, I would have been a Jonah still—not because I have been unlucky for others, but because somebody or something has compelled me to be certain places at certain times, without fail. Conveyances and motives, both conventional and bizarre, have been provided. And, according to plan, at each appointed second, at each appointed place this Jonah was there.

—KURT VONNEGUT, JR., *Cat's Cradle*

My father's family name being Pirrip, and my Christian name Philip, my infant tongue could make of both names nothing longer or more explicit than Pip. So I called myself Pip, and came to be called Pip.

I give Pirrip as my father's family name on the authority

The first page of the original manuscript of Charles Dickens's
Great Expectations. (Wisbech and Fenland Museum)

of his tombstone and my sister—Mrs. Joe Gargery, who married the blacksmith.

—CHARLES DICKENS, *Great Expectations*

You don't know about me, without you have read a book by the name of "The Adventures of Tom Sawyer," but that ain't no matter. That book was made by Mr. Mark Twain, and he told the truth, mainly. There was things which he stretched, but mainly he told the truth. That is nothing. I never seen anybody but lied, one time or another, without it was Aunt Polly, or the widow, or maybe Mary. Aunt Polly—Tom's Aunt Polly, she is—and Mary, and the Widow Douglas, is all told about in that book—which is mostly a true book; with some stretchers, as I said before.

—MARK TWAIN, *Adventures of Huckleberry Finn*

Granted: I am an inmate of a mental hospital; my keeper is watching me, he never lets me out of his sight; there's a peephole in the door, and my keeper's eye is the shade of brown that can never see through a blue-eyed type like me.

So you see, my keeper can't be an enemy. I've come to be very fond of him; when he stops looking at me from behind the door and comes into the room, I tell him incidents from my life, so he can get to know me in spite of the peephole between us.

—GÜNTER GRASS, *The Tin Drum,* trans. Ralph Manheim

For a long time I used to go to bed early. Sometimes, when I had put out my candle, my eyes would close so quickly that I had not even time to say "I'm going to sleep." And half an hour later the thought that it was time to go to sleep would awaken me; I would try to put away the book which, I imagined, was still in my hands, and to blow out the light; I had been thinking all the time, while I was asleep, of what I had just been reading, but my thoughts had run into a channel of their own, until I myself seemed actually to have become the subject of my book: a church, a quartet, the rivalry between François I and Charles V. This impression would persist for some moments after I was awake; it did not disturb my mind, but it lay like scales upon my eyes and prevented them from registering the fact that the candle was no longer burning.

—MARCEL PROUST,
Swann's Way, trans. C. K. Scott Moncrieff

In my younger and more vulnerable years my father gave me some advice that I've been turning over in my mind ever since.

"Whenever you feel like criticizing any one," he told me, "just remember that all the people in this world haven't had the advantages that you've had."

He didn't say any more, but we've always been unusually communicative in a reserved way, and I understood that he

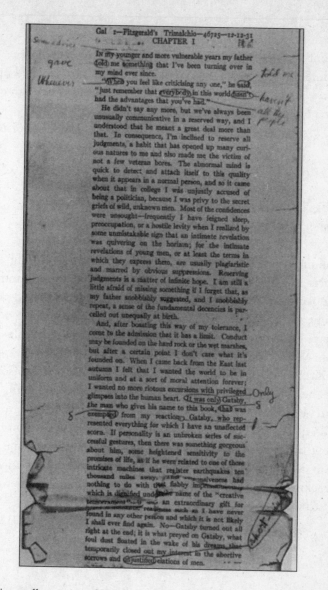

First galley page of F. Scott Fitzgerald's *The Great Gatsby*, with further revisions in hand by the author. (*The Papers of F. Scott Fitzgerald, Manuscripts Division, Department of Rare Books and Special Collections, Princeton University Libraries*)

meant a great deal more than that. In consequence, I'm inclined to reserve all judgments, a habit that has opened up many curious natures to me and also made me the victim of not a few veteran bores.

—F. SCOTT FITZGERALD, *The Great Gatsby*

The Witness as Storyteller ❦
The story through the eyes of a character who acts as narrator.

Call me Ishmael. Some years ago—never mind how long precisely—having little or no money in my purse, and nothing particular to interest me on shore, I thought I would sail about a little and see the watery part of the world. It is a way I have of driving off the spleen, and regulating the circulation. Whenever I find myself growing grim about the mouth; whenever it is a damp, drizzly November in my soul; whenever I find myself involuntarily pausing before coffin warehouses, and bringing up the rear of every funeral I meet; and especially whenever my hypos get such an upper hand of me, that it requires a strong moral principle to prevent me from deliberately stepping into the street, and methodically knocking people's hats off—then, I account it high time to get to sea as soon as I can.

—HERMAN MELVILLE, *Moby-Dick; or, The Whale*

I had the story, bit by bit, from various people, and, as generally happens in such cases, each time it was a different story.

If you know Starkfield, Massachusetts, you know the post-office. If you know the post-office you must have seen Ethan Frome drive up to it, drop the reins on his hollow-backed bay and drag himself across the brick pavement to the white colonnade: and you must have asked who he was.

—EDITH WHARTON, *Ethan Frome*

I first heard of Ántonia on what seemed to me an interminable journey across the great midland plain of North America. I was ten years old then; I had lost both my father and mother within a year, and my Virginia relatives were sending me out to my grandparents, who lived in Nebraska. I travelled in the care of a mountain boy, Jake Marpole, one of the "hands" on my father's old farm under the Blue Ridge, who was now going West to work for my grandfather. Jake's experience of the world was not much wider than mine. He had never been in a railway train until the morning when we set out together to try our fortunes in a new world.

—WILLA CATHER, *My Ántonia*

This is the saddest story I have ever heard. We had known the Ashburnhams for nine seasons of the town of Nauheim with an extreme intimacy—or, rather, with an acquaintanceship as loose and easy and yet as close as a good glove's with

your hand. My wife and I knew Captain and Mrs. Ashburnham as well as it was possible to know anybody, and yet, in
another sense, we knew nothing at all about them. This is, I
believe, a state of things only possible with English people of
whom, till today, when I sit down to puzzle out what I
know of this sad affair, I knew nothing whatever.

—FORD MADOX FORD, *The Good Soldier*

1801.—I have just returned from a visit to my landlord—the
solitary neighbour that I shall be troubled with. This is certainly, a beautiful country! In all England, I do not believe
that I could have fixed on a situation so completely removed
from the stir of society. A perfect misanthropist's Heaven—
and Mr Heathcliff and I are such a suitable pair to divide the
desolation between us. A capital fellow! He little imagined
how my heart warmed towards him when I beheld his black
eyes withdraw so suspiciously under their brows, as I rode
up, and when his fingers sheltered themselves, with a jealous
resolution, still further in his waistcoat, as I announced my
name.

'Mr Heathcliff?' I said.

A nod was the answer.

—EMILY BRONTË, *Wuthering Heights*

We were in class when the headmaster came in, followed by
a new boy, not wearing the school uniform, and a school
servant carrying a large desk. Those who had been asleep

woke up, and every one rose as if just surprised at his work.

The headmaster made a sign to us to sit down. Then, turning to the teacher, he said to him in a low voice:

"Monsieur Roger, here is a pupil whom I recommend to your care; he'll be in the second. If his work and conduct are satisfactory, he will go into one of the upper classes, as becomes his age."

—GUSTAVE FLAUBERT, *Madame Bovary,* trans. Paul de Man, based on version by Eleanor Marx Aveling

3 ❧ THE AUTHOR INTRUDES

t was common for nineteenth-century novelists to address their readers directly—usually as "dear reader"—to tell them what to expect from the story that was to follow, or what their own feelings or limitations were in writing it. Such an intrusion placed them above and apart from their characters, a relationship that brings to mind the Hirshfeld cartoon for the stage production of *My Fair Lady,* which depicted Bernard Shaw manipulating Henry Higgins and Eliza Doolittle on marionette strings. In the drawing, Shaw looks suspiciously like God, and in a sense, the author acts as God when he intrudes on the story he is telling: he reminds us that *he* or *she* is the Creator of the characters we are about to meet.

Although this approach is not used as often today, it still has the same effect: it gives the "dear reader" the feeling that the author has placed an arm around his shoulder, and is about to confide something to him alone. "With a single drop of ink for a mirror, the Egyptian sorcerer undertakes to reveal to any chance comer far-reaching visions of the past. This is what I undertake to do for you, reader," begins George Eliot's *Adam Bede*. Once the reader is in the author's confidence and the story or the hero has been introduced, the intimacy of the first person is abandoned, and the story begins to move on its own.

Sometimes the author masks himself by assuming the identity of another, fictional "writer," as Robert Louis Stevenson did in *Treasure Island*: "Squire Trelawney, Dr. Livesey, and the rest of these gentlemen having asked me to write down the whole particulars about Treasure Island, from the beginning to the end, keeping nothing back but the bearings of the island, and that only because there is still treasure not yet lifted, I take up my pen in the year of grace 17—..." Or the author pretends to be the discoverer of a manuscript written by someone else. "The writer of this singular autobiography was my cousin, who died at the ———— Criminal Lunatic Asylum, of which he had been an inmate three years," begins George du Maurier's *Peter Ibbetson*. The faux-author is simply an "editor," and usually takes pains to disclaim responsibility for the contents, as well as for the quality, of the writing. Thus we can enjoy the irony of Conrad, the consummate stylist, writing, in *Under Western Eyes*: "To begin with I wish to disclaim the possession of those high gifts of imagination and expression which would have enabled my pen to create for the reader the personality of the man who called himself, after the Russian custom, Cyril son of Isidor—Kirylo Sidorovitch—Razumov."

Frequently, the author's statement of his intentions for the novel, or the faux-author's introduction of the manuscript, journal, or letters on which the novel is based, is kept to a preface (or "prologue" or "introduction" as it is called in *Peter Ibbetson*). As distinguished from the prefatory note written and signed by the author, this preface is a part of the novel, and adds valuable information to the story. It is the author playing hide-and-seek with his reader.

The Author and Faux-Author 🦋

The author introduces his story—as himself and in disguise as another.

I have never begun a novel with more misgiving. If I call it a novel it is only because I don't know what else to call it. I have little story to tell and I end neither with a death nor a marriage. Death ends all things and so is the comprehensive conclusion of a story, but marriage finishes it very properly too and the sophisticated are ill-advised to sneer at what is by convention termed a happy ending. It is a sound instinct of the common people which persuades them that with this all that needs to be said is said. When male and female, after whatever vicissitudes you like, are at last brought together they have fulfilled their biological function and interest passes to the generation that is to come. But I leave my reader in the air. This book consists of my recollections of a man with whom I was thrown into close contact only at long intervals, and I have little knowledge of what happened to him in between. I suppose that by the exercise of invention I could fill the gaps plausibly enough and so make my narrative more coherent; but I have no wish to do that. I only want to set down what I know of my own knowledge.

—W. SOMERSET MAUGHAM, *The Razor's Edge*

With a single drop of ink for a mirror, the Egyptian sorcerer undertakes to reveal to any chance comer far-reaching visions of the past. This is what I undertake to do for you, reader. With this drop of ink at the end of my pen, I will show you the roomy workshop of Mr. Jonathan Burge, carpenter and builder, in the village of Hayslope, as it appeared on the eighteenth of June, in the year of our Lord 1799.

—GEORGE ELIOT, *Adam Bede*

This is a true story but I can't believe it's really happening.

It's a murder story, too. I can't believe my luck.

And a love story (I think), of all strange things, so late in the century, so late in the goddamned day.

—MARTIN AMIS, *London Fields*

To begin with I wish to disclaim the possession of those high gifts of imagination and expression which would have enabled my pen to create for the reader the personality of the man who called himself, after the Russian custom, Cyril son of Isidor—Kirylo Sidorovitch—Razumov.

If I have ever had these gifts in any sort of living form they have been smothered out of existence a long time ago under a wilderness of words. Words, as is well known, are the great foes of reality. I have been for many years a teacher of languages. It is an occupation which at length becomes fatal to whatever share of imagination, observation, and insight an ordinary person may be heir to. To a teacher of languages there comes a time when the world is but a place of many words and man appears a mere talking animal not much more wonderful than a parrot.

—JOSEPH CONRAD, *Under Western Eyes*

Squire Trelawney, Dr. Livesey, and the rest of these gentlemen having asked me to write down the whole particulars about Treasure Island, from the beginning to the end, keeping nothing back but the bearings of the island, and that only because there is still treasure not yet lifted, I take up my pen in the year of grace 17— and go back to the time when my father kept the Admiral Benbow inn and the brown old seaman with the sabre cut first took up his lodging under our roof.

I remember him as if it were yesterday, as he came plodding to the inn door, his sea-chest following behind him in a hand-barrow—a tall, strong, heavy, nut-brown

man, his tarry pigtail falling over the shoulders of his soiled
blue coat, his hands ragged and scarred, with black, broken
nails, and the sabre cut across one cheek, a dirty, livid
white.

—ROBERT LOUIS STEVENSON, *Treasure Island*

The first ray of light which illumines the gloom, and con-
verts into a dazzling brilliancy that obscurity in which the
earlier history of the public career of the immortal Pickwick
would appear to be involved, is derived from the perusal of
the following entry in the Transactions of the Pickwick
Club, which the editor of these papers feels the highest pleasure in laying before his readers as a proof of the careful
attention, indefatigable assiduity, and nice discrimination
with which his search among the multi-farious documents
confided to him has been conducted.

   "May 12, 1827. Joseph Smiggers, Esq., P.V.P.M.P.C.,*
presiding. The following resolutions unanimously
agreed to:"

*Perpetual Vice-President—Member Pickwick Club.

—CHARLES DICKENS, *The Posthumous Papers
of the Pickwick Club*

Editors' Note
These notebooks were found among the papers of Antoine
Roquentin. They are published without alteration.
   The first sheet is undated, but there is good reason to

believe it was written some weeks before the diary itself. Thus it would have been written around the beginning of January, 1932, at the latest.

At that time, Antoine Roquentin, after travelling through Central Europe, North Africa and the Far East, settled in Bouville for three years to conclude his historical research on the Marquis de Rollebon.

The Editors
—JEAN-PAUL SARTRE, Nausea,
trans. Lloyd Alexander

I had this story from one who had no business to tell it to me, or to any other. I may credit the seductive influence of an old vintage upon the narrator for the beginning of it, and my own skeptical incredulity during the days that followed for the balance of the strange tale.

When my convivial host discovered that he had told me so much, and that I was prone to doubtfulness, his foolish pride assumed the task the old vintage had commenced, and so he unearthed written evidence in the form of musty manuscript, and dry official records of the British Colonial Office, to support many of the salient features of his remarkable narrative.

—EDGAR RICE BURROUGHS,
Tarzan of the Apes

4 &8 ENTER THE HERO/HEROINE

lthough a novel can be suggested by a situation or a setting, it is more likely to come about because of a character the writer conceives as a hero or heroine. Whether the character bears a resemblance to the writer, in looks, traits, or beliefs, or conversely, is the kind of person the writer secretly admires (or despises), the hero/heroine exists because he or she has a personal significance to the author. For the novelist, identifying the bond that has drawn him to a particular hero or heroine is particularly important in clarifying the passion that will move the book. The bond may be a strongly held belief, a common background, a sense of rebellion against life, a shared strength or weakness, but it must be relevant to the novelist for the character's essence to be communicated to the reader.

Often, the bond is love. For instance, the heroine of

Thomas Hardy's *A Pair of Blue Eyes* is drawn from his first wife, Emma Lavinia Gifford, and his *Tess of the d'Urbervilles* from a chance sighting of a Dorset milkmaid who captivated him. The impression was so strong that when, in his dotage, Hardy saw Tess come to life in a young actress portraying her in a local dramatization of the novel (the daughter of a woman who had worked at the same farm and, conceivably, "Tess's" daughter), he began an obsessive relationship with his own character, a relationship that his (second, much younger) wife jealously brought to an end.

The lifelikeness of a heroine like Hardy's Tess is one of the distinguishing characteristics of the modern novel. The romantic heroes and heroines of the eighteenth century bore as little resemblance to reality as did the world of melodrama and adventure they inhabited. As the novel progressed into the nineteenth century, however, these cardboard creations matured into living, believable characters who moved in realistic situations. Such characters may not be precisely true to life—a hero or heroine can be *more* noble or evil than a real-life counterpart might be expected to be—but they should act in a manner that is consistent and believable for that character.

Because the writer is so personally involved with the principal character, it is natural that many novels begin with a description of the hero or heroine. In fact, the first words of the novel are often the hero's name. "Scarlett O'Hara was not beautiful"; "Emma Woodhouse, handsome, clever, and rich"; "The Miss Lonelyhearts of the New York *Post-Dispatch*"; "Robert Cohn was once middleweight boxing champion of Princeton"; "Roy Hobbs pawed at the glass" all give the hero/heroine the first entrance. The same technique can also introduce a secondary character, or even a character whose only importance is establishing the setting for the book.

Cynthia Turned, Her Eyes Smouldering ❦
The immediate introduction of one or more of the book's main characters.

Scarlett O'Hara was not beautiful, but men seldom realized it when caught by her charm as the Tarleton twins were. In her face were too sharply blended the delicate features of her mother, a Coast aristocrat of French descent, and the heavy ones of her florid Irish father. But it was an arresting face, pointed of chin, square of jaw. Her eyes were pale green without a touch of hazel, starred with bristly black lashes and slightly tilted at the ends. Above them, her thick black brows slanted upward, cutting a startling oblique line in her magnolia-white skin—that skin so prized by Southern women and so carefully guarded with bonnets, veils and mittens against hot Georgia suns.

—MARGARET MITCHELL, *Gone With the Wind*

Robert Cohn was once middleweight boxing champion of Princeton. Do not think that I am very much impressed by that as a boxing title, but it meant a lot to Cohn. He cared nothing for boxing, in fact he disliked it, but he learned it painfully and thoroughly to counteract the feeling of inferiority and shyness he had felt on being treated as a Jew at Princeton. There was a certain inner comfort in knowing he could knock down anybody who was snooty to him, although, being very shy and a thoroughly nice boy, he never fought except in the gym.

—ERNEST HEMINGWAY, *The Sun Also Rises*

Emma Woodhouse, handsome, clever, and rich, with a comfortable home and happy disposition, seemed to unite some of the best blessings of existence, and had lived nearly twenty-one years in the world with very little to distress or vex her.

—JANE AUSTEN, *Emma*

Mr. Sherlock Holmes, who was usually very late in the mornings, save upon those not infrequent occasions when he was up all night, was seated at the breakfast table. I stood upon the hearth-rug and picked up the stick which our visitor had left behind him the night before. It was a fine, thick piece of wood, bulbous-headed, of the sort which is known as a "Penang lawyer."

—SIR ARTHUR CONAN DOYLE, *The Hound of the Baskervilles*

Mr. Phileas Fogg lived, in 1872, at No. 7, Savile Row, Burlington Gardens, the house in which Sheridan died in 1814. He was one of the most noticeable members of the

Reform Club, though he seemed always to avoid attracting attention; an enigmatical personage, about whom little was known, except that he was a polished man of the world. People said that he resembled Byron,—at least that his head was Byronic; but he was a bearded, tranquil Byron, who might live on a thousand years without growing old.

—JULES VERNE, *Around the World in Eighty Days,*
trans. George Makepeace Towle

Alexey Fyodorovitch Karamazov was the third son of Fyodor Pavlovitch Karamazov, a landowner well known in our district in his own day, and still remembered among us owing to his gloomy and tragic death, which happened thirteen years ago, and which I shall describe in its proper place. For the present I will only say that this "landowner"—for so we used to call him, although he hardly spent a day of his life on his own estate—was a strange type, yet one pretty frequently to be met with, a type abject and vicious and at the same time senseless. But he was one of those senseless persons who are very well capable of looking after their worldly affairs, and, apparently, after nothing else.

—FYODOR DOSTOYEVSKY, *The Brothers Karamazov,*
trans. Constance Garnett

Lolita, light of my life, fire of my loins. My sin, my soul. Lo-lee-ta: the tip of the tongue taking a trip of three steps down the palate to tap, at three, on the teeth. Lo. Lee. Ta.

First page of the (apparently) complete manuscript version of
H. G. Wells's *The Time Machine*. *(The University of Illinois at
Urbana-Champaign)*

She was Lo, plain Lo, in the morning, standing four feet ten in one sock. She was Lola in slacks. She was Dolly at school. She was Dolores on the dotted line. But in my arms she was always Lolita.

—VLADIMIR NABOKOV, *Lolita*

The Time Traveller (for so it will be convenient to speak of him) was expounding a recondite matter to us. His grey eyes shone and twinkled, and his usually pale face was flushed and animated. The fire burned brightly, and the soft radiance of the incandescent lights in the lilies of silver caught the bubbles that flashed and passed in our glasses.

—H. G. WELLS, *The Time Machine*

Ursula and Gudrun Brangwen sat one morning in the window-bay of their father's house in Beldover, working and talking. Ursula was stitching a piece of brightly-coloured embroidery, and Gudrun was drawing upon a board which she held on her knee. They were mostly silent, talking as their thoughts strayed through their minds.

"Ursula," said Gudrun, "don't you *really want* to get married?"

—D. H. LAWRENCE, *Women in Love*

Standing amid the tan, excited post-Christmas crowd at the Southwest Florida Regional Airport, Rabbit Angstrom has a funny sudden feeling that what he has come to meet, what's floating in unseen about to land, is not his son Nelson and daughter-in-law Pru and their two children but something more ominous and intimately his: his own death, shaped vaguely like an airplane.

—JOHN UPDIKE, *Rabbit at Rest*

Riding up the winding road of Saint Agnes Cemetery in the back of the rattling old truck, Francis Phelan became aware that the dead, even more than the living, settled down in neighborhoods. The truck was suddenly surrounded by fields of monuments and cenotaphs of kindred design and striking size, all guarding the privileged dead.

—WILLIAM KENNEDY, *Ironweed*

When Farmer Oak smiled, the corners of his mouth spread till they were within an unimportant distance of his ears, his eyes were reduced to mere chinks, and diverging wrinkles appeared round them, extending upon his countenance like the rays in a rudimentary sketch of the rising sun.

His Christian name was Gabriel, and on working days he was a young man of sound judgment, easy motions, proper dress, and general good character. On Sundays he was a man of misty views, rather given to postponing, and hampered by his best clothes and umbrella: upon the whole, one who felt himself to occupy morally that vast middle space of Laodicean neutrality which lay between the Communion people of the parish and the drunken section,—that is, he went to church, but yawned privately by the time the congregation reached the Nicene creed, and thought of what there would be for dinner when he meant to be listening to the sermon.

—THOMAS HARDY, *Far from the Madding Crowd*

Bizarre as was the name she bore, Kim Ravenal always said she was thankful it had been no worse. She knew whereof she spoke, for it was literally by a breath that she had escaped being called Mississippi.

"Imagine Mississippi Ravenal!" she often said, in later years. "They'd have cut it to Missy, I suppose, or even Sippy, if you can bear to think of anything so horrible. And then I'd have had to change my name or give up the stage altogether. Because who'd go to see—seriously, I mean—an actress named Sippy? It sounds half-witted, for some reason. Kim's bad enough, God knows."

—EDNA FERBER, *Show Boat*

Mr. Tench went out to look for his ether cylinder: out into the blazing Mexican sun and the bleaching dust. A few buzzards looked down from the roof with shabby indifference: he wasn't carrion yet. A faint feeling of rebellion stirred in Mr. Tench's heart, and he wrenched up a piece of the road with splintering finger-nails and tossed it feebly up at them.

—GRAHAM GREENE, *The Power and the Glory*

5 ❧ THE IMPERSONAL PRONOUN

elying on only the personal pronoun to introduce a character is like dropping a scrim curtain
in front of a scene on the stage: we see the action
perfectly well, but the identity of the faces is hidden from us until the stage manager permits the curtain to
rise. The effect is also the same: an enhanced sense of drama
and mystery: "He awoke, opened his eyes. The room meant
very little to him; he was too deeply immersed in the non-
being from which he had just come" (Paul Bowles, *The Sheltering Sky*).

Witholding the name of a character who begins a book,
whether principal or subordinate, gained popularity as the
novel moved into the twentieth century. Beginning a novel
with "he" or "she" allowed the author to involve the reader in
a description or action of the character without the somewhat
artificial, self-conscious use of the proper name. It especially

suited the short-sentenced, blunt style of writers like Hemingway, although it had of course been used effectively by authors like Conrad in *Lord Jim,* and Kipling in *Kim.* In expert hands like these, the technique was dramatic, powerful, almost poetic.

Impersonally Speaking ❦
We learn where and what the character is, before we learn who he or she is.

He lay flat on the brown, pine-needled floor of the forest, his chin on his folded arms, and high overhead the wind blew in the tops of the pine trees. The mountainside sloped gently where he lay; but below it was steep and he could see the dark of the oiled road winding through the pass. There was a stream alongside the road and far down the pass he saw a mill beside the stream and the falling water of the dam, white in the summer sunlight.

—ERNEST HEMINGWAY, *For Whom the Bell Tolls*

He was an inch, perhaps two, under six feet, powerfully built, and he advanced straight at you with a slight stoop of the shoulders, head forward, and a fixed from-under stare which made you think of a charging bull. His voice was deep, loud, and his manner displayed a kind of dogged self-assertion which had nothing aggressive in it. It seemed a necessity, and it was directed apparently as much at himself as at anybody else. He was spotlessly neat, apparelled in immaculate white from shoes to hat, and in the various Eastern ports where he got his living as ship-chandler's water-clerk he was very popular.

—JOSEPH CONRAD, *Lord Jim*

She was so deeply imbedded in my consciousness that for the first year of school I seem to have believed that each of my teachers was my mother in disguise. As soon as the last bell had sounded, I would rush off for home, wondering as I ran if I could possibly make it to our apartment before she had succeeded in transforming herself. Invariably she was already in the kitchen by the time I arrived, and setting out my milk and cookies.

—PHILIP ROTH, *Portnoy's Complaint*

A bird cried out on the roof, and he woke up. It was the middle of the afternoon, in the heat, in Africa; he knew at once where he was. Not even in the suspended seconds between sleep and waking was he left behind in the house in Wiltshire, lying, now, deep in the snow of a hard winter.

—NADINE GORDIMER, *A Guest of Honour*

He awoke, opened his eyes. The room meant very little to him; he was too deeply immersed in the non-being from which he had just come. If he had not the energy to ascertain his position in time and space, he also lacked the desire.

He was somewhere, he had come back through vast regions from nowhere; there was the certitude of an infinite sadness at the core of his consciousness, but the sadness was reassuring, because it alone was familiar.

—PAUL BOWLES, *The Sheltering Sky*

He sat, in defiance of municipal orders, astride the gun Zam-Zammah on her brick platform opposite the old Ajaib-Gher—the Wonder House, as the natives called the Lahore Museum. Who hold Zam-Zammah, that 'fire-breathing dragon,' hold the Punjab; for the great green-bronze piece is always first of the conqueror's loot.

—RUDYARD KIPLING, *Kim*

He was born with a gift of laughter and a sense that the world was mad. And that was all his patrimony. His very paternity was obscure, although the village of Gavrillac had long since dispelled the cloud of mystery that hung about it. Those simple Brittany folk were not so simple as to be deceived by a pretended relationship which did not even possess the virtue of originality. When a nobleman, for no apparent reason, announces himself the godfather of an infant fetched no man knew whence, and thereafter cares for the lad's rearing and education, the most unsophisticated of country folk perfectly understand the situation.

—RAFAEL SABATINI, *Scaramouche*

He was an old man who fished alone in a skiff in the Gulf Stream and he had gone eighty-four days now without taking a fish. In the first forty days a boy had been with him. But after forty days without a fish the boy's parents had told him that the old man was now definitely and finally *salao*, which is the worst form of unlucky, and the boy had gone at their orders in another boat which caught three good fish the first week. It made the boy sad to see the old man come in each day with his skiff empty and he always went down to help him carry either the coiled lines or the gaff and harpoon and the sail that was furled around the mast. The sail was patched with flour sacks and, furled, it looked like the flag of permanent defeat.

—ERNEST HEMINGWAY, *The Old Man and the Sea*

6 ❧ SETTING THE SETTING

ew elements of the novel perform as many useful and important functions as the setting. The setting lifts us out of the world we know to a different time and place so that we can experience a period, a culture, a country that might be completely alien to us. It sets the stage for the drama that is to unfold, and prepares us to understand why a character acts the way he does. It can create a mood so strong that it almost becomes another character in the story, pushing the hero helplessly to his fate, or challenging him to struggle against it. It can be a symbol of the hero's strength, as Tara is to Scarlett O'Hara in *Gone With the Wind*. Even if the setting is unobtrusive or ordinary, as it is in many contemporary novels like those of Ann Beattie and John Updike, it can make a point by emphasizing the banality of that everyday life. No matter what its function, however, the novel must have a setting; it is up to the author to decide what use he wishes to make of it.

When the setting begins a book, it assumes a dramatic prominence, emphasizing the importance to the author of the geographic or cultural or atmospheric elements that will influence the action. When John Steinbeck begins, "The Salinas Valley is in Northern California," he sets the boundaries for the characters of *East of Eden.* When Henry James writes in *The American,* "On a brilliant day in May, in the year 1868, a gentleman was reclining at his ease on the great circular divan which at that period occupied the centre of the Salon Carré, in the Museum of the Louvre," he indicates not just a time in space, but the cultural ambiance we are to expect. When Thomas Hardy relates, "A Saturday afternoon in November was approaching the time of twilight, and the vast tract of unenclosed wild known as Egdon Heath embrowned itself moment by moment," he is introducing a landscape that is to be an omnipresent force in *The Return of the Native.*

For Hardy, the dark heaths, the wild, high-cliffed coastline, the hedge-rowed farmland, the clustered thatch-roofed cottages of England's West Country provided all three of these important functions of the setting; in his novels he seldom needed to stray far from home. So, too, William Faulkner, Sarah Orne Jewett, and D. H. Lawrence give us, in novel after novel, detailed glimpses into the South, the New England town, the north of England. Sometimes a fictional name thinly masks an actual location, like Hardy's Wessex or Faulkner's Yoknapatawpha County, but the reality of the setting shines through clearly, placing and influencing the characters, and convincing us that we are there.

The selections in this chapter illustrate the three major elements of setting: Geography, Time, and Weather. The first, although it may appear to be nothing more than description, is actually giving us vital information, directly or indirectly, about the location that will be central to the story. "Except for the Marabar Caves ..." begins Forster's *A Passage to India,* quickly passing by us what we will discover to be the focus of the novel. The second is preparing us to enter a particular place at a particular time. "While the present century was in its teens, and on one sunshiny morning in June, there drove up to the great iron gate of Miss Pinkerton's academy for young ladies, on Chiswick Mall, a large family coach ..." writes Thackeray in *Vanity Fair.* We abandon the present to travel with the author backward, or in the case of authors like H. G. Wells, forward, in space. The last, the element of Weather, provides the atmosphere and the mood of the story or the principal character. "The cold passed reluctantly from the earth, and the retiring fogs revealed an army stretched out on the hills, resting," opens Stephen Crane's *The Red Badge of Courage,* painting a gray setting for his episode of the Civil War.

The Scene Is Set ❧

The author places the story geographically.

Except for the Marabar Caves—and they are twenty miles off—the city of Chandrapore presents nothing extraordinary. Edged rather than washed by the River Ganges, it trails for a couple of miles along the bank, scarcely distinguishable from the rubbish it deposits so freely. There are no bathing-steps on the river front, as the Ganges happens not to be holy here; indeed there is no river front, and bazaars shut out the wide and shifting panorama of the stream. The streets are mean, the temples ineffective, and though a few fine houses exist they are hidden away in gardens or down alleys whose filth deters all but the invited guest.

—E. M. FORSTER, *A Passage to India*

Half-way down a by-street of one of our New England towns stands a rusty wooden house, with seven acutely peaked gables, facing towards various points of the compass, and a huge, clustered chimney in the midst. The street is Pyncheon Street; the house is the old Pyncheon House; and an elm-tree, of wide circumference, rooted before the door, is familiar to every town-born child by the title of the Pyncheon Elm. On my occasional visits to the town aforesaid, I seldom failed to turn down Pyncheon Street, for the sake of passing through the shadow of these two antiquities,—the great elm-tree and the weather-beaten edifice.

—NATHANIEL HAWTHORNE, *The House of the Seven Gables*

Paint me a small railroad station then, ten minutes before dark. Beyond the platform are the waters of the Wekonsett River, reflecting a somber afterglow. The architecture of the station is oddly informal, gloomy but unserious, and mostly resembles a pergola, cottage or summer house although this is a climate of harsh winters. The lamps along the platform burn with a nearly palpable plaintiveness. The setting seems in some way to be at the heart of the matter.

—JOHN CHEEVER, *Bullet Park*

Imagine, then, a flat landscape, dark for the moment, but even so conveying to a girl running in the still deeper shadow cast by the wall of the Bibighar Gardens an idea of immensity, of distance, such as years before Miss Crane had been conscious of standing where a lane ended and cultivation began: a different landscape but also in the alluvial plain between the mountains of the north and the plateau of the south.

It is a landscape which a few hours ago, between the rainfall and the short twilight, extracted colour from the spectrum of the setting sun and dyed every one of its own surfaces that could absorb light: the ochre walls of the houses in the old town (which are stained too with their bloody past and uneasy present); the moving water of the river and the still water of the tanks; the shiny stubble, the ploughed earth, of distant fields; the metal of the grand trunk road. In this landscape trees are sparse, except among the white bungalows of the civil lines. On the horizon there is a violet smudge of hill country.

—PAUL SCOTT, *The Jewel in the Crown*

There is a lovely road that runs from Ixopo into the hills. These hills are grass-covered and rolling, and they are lovely beyond any singing of it. The road climbs seven miles into them, to Carisbrooke; and from there, if there is no mist, you look down on one of the fairest valleys of Africa. About you there is grass and bracken and you may hear the forlorn crying of the titihoya, one of the birds of the veld. Below you is the valley of the Umzimkulu, on its journey from the Drakensberg to the sea; and beyond and behind the river, great hill after great hill; and beyond and behind them, the mountains of Ingeli and East Griqualand.

—ALAN PATON, *Cry, the Beloved Country*

The Salinas Valley is in Northern California. It is a long narrow swale between two ranges of mountains, and the Salinas River winds and twists up the center until it falls at last into Monterey Bay.

—JOHN STEINBECK, *East of Eden*

A few miles south of Soledad, the Salinas River drops in close to the hillside bank and runs deep and green. The water is warm too, for it has slipped twinkling over the yellow sands in the sunlight before reaching the narrow pool. On one side of the river the golden foothill slopes curve up to the strong and rocky Gabilan mountains, but on the valley side the water is lined with trees—willows fresh and green with every spring, carrying in their lower leaf junctures the debris of the winter's flooding; and sycamores with mottled, white, recumbent limbs and branches that arch over the pool.

—JOHN STEINBECK, *Of Mice and Men*

Two mountain chains traverse the republic roughly from north to south, forming between them a number of valleys and plateaus. Overlooking one of these valleys, which is dominated by two volcanoes, lies, six thousand feet above sea level, the town of Quauhnahuac. It is situated well south of the Tropic of Cancer, to be exact on the nineteenth parallel, in about the same latitude as the Revillagigedo Islands to the west in the Pacific, or very much further west, the southernmost tip of Hawaii—and as the port of Tzucox to the east on the Atlantic seaboard of Yucatan near the border of British Honduras, or very much further east, the town of Juggernaut, in India, on the Bay of Bengal.

—MALCOLM LOWRY, *Under the Volcano*

LANDSCAPE-TONES: brown to bronze, steep skyline, low cloud, pearl ground with shadowed oyster and violet reflections. The lion-dust of desert: prophets' tombs turned to zinc and copper at sunset on the ancient lake. Its huge sand-faults like watermarks from the air; green and citron giving to gunmetal, to a single plum-dark sail, moist, palpitant:

sticky-winged nymph. Taposiris is dead among its tumbling columns and seamarks, vanished the Harpoon Men ... Mareotis under a sky of hot lilac.

—LAWRENCE DURRELL, *Balthazar*

Time and Time Again 🦗
The writer takes us to a specific time and place.

While the present century was in its teens, and on one sunshiny morning in June, there drove up to the great iron gate of Miss Pinkerton's academy for young ladies, on Chiswick Mall, a large family coach, with two fat horses in blazing harness, driven by a fat coachman in a three-cornered hat and wig, at the rate of four miles an hour.

—WILLIAM MAKEPEACE THACKERAY, *Vanity Fair*

On Friday noon, July the twentieth, 1714, the finest bridge in all Peru broke and precipitated five travellers into the gulf below. This bridge was on the high-road between Lima and Cuzco and hundreds of persons passed over it every day. It had been woven of osier by the Incas more than a century before and visitors to the city were always led out to see it. It was a mere ladder of thin slats swung out over the gorge, with hand-rails of dried vine.

—THORNTON WILDER, *The Bridge of San Luis Rey*

It is cold at 6:40 in the morning of a March day in Paris, and seems even colder when a man is about to be executed by firing squad. At that hour on March 11, 1963, in the main courtyard of the Fort d'Ivry a French Air Force colonel stood before a stake driven into the chilly gravel as his hands were bound behind the post, and stared with slowly diminishing disbelief at the squad of soldiers facing him twenty metres away.

—FREDERICK FORSYTH, *The Day of the Jackal*

No one would have believed in the last years of the nineteenth century that this world was being watched keenly and closely by intelligences greater than man's and yet as mortal as his own; that as men busied themselves about their various concerns they were scrutinised and studied, perhaps almost as narrowly as a man with a microscope might scrutinise the transient creatures that swarm and multiply in a drop of water. With infinite complacency men went to and fro over this globe about their little affairs, serene in their assurance of their empire over matter.

—H. G. WELLS, *The War of the Worlds*

It was June, 1933, one week after Commencement, when Kay Leiland Strong, Vassar '33, the first of her class to run around the table at the Class Day dinner, was married to Harald Petersen, Reed '27, in the chapel of St. George's Church, P.E., Karl F. Reiland, Rector. Outside, on

Stuyvesant Square, the trees were in full leaf, and the wedding guests arriving by twos and threes in taxis heard the voices of children playing round the statue of Peter Stuyvesant in the park.

—MARY MCCARTHY, *The Group*

In the year 1815 Monseigneur Charles-François-Bienvenu Myriel was Bishop of Digne. He was then about seventy-five, having held the bishopric since 1806.

Although it has no direct bearing on the tale we have to tell, we must nevertheless give some account of the rumours and gossip concerning him which were in circulation when he came to occupy the diocese.

—VICTOR HUGO, *Les Misérables*, trans. Norman Denny

On February 24, 1815, the watchtower at Marseilles signaled the arrival of the three-master *Pharaon*, coming from Smyrna, Trieste and Naples.

The quay was soon covered with the usual crowd of curious onlookers, for the arrival of a ship is always a great event in Marseilles, especially when, like the *Pharaon*, it has been built, rigged and laden in the city and belongs to a local shipowner.

—ALEXANDRE DUMAS, *The Count of Monte Cristo*,
trans. Lowell Bair

The unusual events described in this chronicle occurred in 194— at Oran. Everyone agreed that, considering their somewhat extraordinary character, they were out of place there. For its ordinariness is what strikes one first about the town of Oran, which is merely a large French port on the Algerian coast, headquarters of the Prefect of a French Department.

—ALBERT CAMUS, *The Plague*, trans. Stuart Gilbert

It Was a Dark and Stormy Night 🎋
The weather sets the mood of the story.

There was no possibility of taking a walk that day. We had been wandering, indeed, in the leafless shrubbery an hour in the morning; but since dinner (Mrs. Reed, when there was no company, dined early) the cold winter wind had brought with it clouds so sombre, and a rain so penetrating, that further outdoor exercise was now out of the question.

—CHARLOTTE BRONTË, *Jane Eyre*

To the red country and part of the gray country of Oklahoma, the last rains came gently, and they did not cut the scarred earth. The plows crossed and recrossed the rivulet marks. The last rains lifted the corn quickly and scattered weed colonies and grass along the sides of the roads so that the gray country and the dark red country began to disappear under a green cover. In the last part of May the sky grew pale and the clouds that had hung in high puffs for so long in the spring were dissipated. The sun flared down on the growing corn day after day until a line of brown spread along the edge of each green bayonet. The clouds appeared, and went away, and in a while they did not try any more. The weeds grew darker green to protect themselves, and they did not spread any more. The surface of the earth crusted, a thin hard crust, and as the sky became pale, so the earth became pale, pink in the red country and white in the gray country.

—JOHN STEINBECK, *The Grapes of Wrath*

A Saturday afternoon in November was approaching the time of twilight, and the vast tract of unenclosed wild known as Egdon Heath embrowned itself moment by moment. Overhead the hollow stretch of whitish cloud shutting out the sky was as a tent which had the whole heath for its floor.

—THOMAS HARDY, *The Return of the Native*

To-day a rare sun of spring. And horse carts clanging to the quays down Tara Street and the shoeless white-faced kids screaming.

—J. P. DONLEAVY, *The Ginger Man*

The first page of the original manuscript of John Steinbeck's *The Grapes of Wrath*. *(John Steinbeck Collection [#6239], Clifton Waller Barrett Library, University of Virginia Library)*

The cold passed reluctantly from the earth, and the retiring fogs revealed an army stretched out on the hills, resting. As the landscape changed from brown to green, the army awakened, and began to tremble with eagerness at the noise of rumors. It cast its eyes upon the roads, which were growing from long troughs of liquid mud to proper thoroughfares. A river, amber-tinted in the shadow of its banks, purled at the army's feet; and at night, when the stream had become of a sorrowful blackness, one could see across it the red, eyelike gleam of hostile camp-fires set in the low brows of distant hills.

—STEPHEN CRANE, *The Red Badge of Courage*

The sun had not yet risen. The sea was indistinguishable from the sky, except that the sea was slightly creased as if a cloth had wrinkles in it. Gradually as the sky whitened a dark line lay on the horizon dividing the sea from the sky and the grey cloth became barred with thick strokes moving, one after another, beneath the surface, following each other, pursuing each other, perpetually.

—VIRGINIA WOOLF, *The Waves*

The sea which lies before me as I write glows rather than sparkles in the bland May sunshine. With the tide turning, it leans quietly against the land, almost unflecked by ripples or by foam. Near to the horizon it is a luxurious purple, spotted with regular lines of emerald green. At the horizon it is indigo. Near to the shore, where my view is framed by rising heaps of humpy yellow rock, there is a band of lighter green, icy and pure, less radiant, opaque however, not transparent.

—IRIS MURDOCH, *The Sea, The Sea*

7 ❧ THE PLOT'S THE THING

match strikes, a gun reports, reveille sounds, something is happening.

The decision to begin a story with action is to a large extent a defensive one: a reader not caught by the first page is probably a lost reader. There are exceptions of course, novels where the power of the author's reputation or the book's critical acclaim will induce him to hold on, but for the most part, today's reader has neither time nor patience for long, leisured Jamesian beginnings.

The alternative is to start with Something Happening, preferably something unusual or shocking. As we open Larry McMurtry's *Lonesome Dove,* the action, if rather repugnant, is nevertheless fascinating: "When Augustus came out on the porch the blue pigs were eating a rattlesnake—not a very big one." The sentence pretty well guarantees the reader will read on—at least to the next sentence.

If the action is more than an isolated arresting episode, but is intrinsic to the plot, all the better. So we find novels that begin with crowd scenes, novels that begin with deaths, novels that begin with journeys; the plot is already in motion. (Boris Pasternak managed to combine both a death *and* a journey in *Doctor Zhivago,* with the funeral procession of Zhivago's wife.) These active openings carry their own excitement with them. Before we finish the first sentence, we are already asking the question every novelist must keep in the mind of his reader until the final page: "What is going to happen next?"

Mystery is at the heart of any successful plot, and in a novel as in life, nothing intrigues our curiosity as much as the arrival of an unidentified stranger. Often the catalyst to the story, the stranger appeals to our human voyeuristic tendencies, and we are prepared to hear more when novelists as diverse as Dostoyevsky, Sinclair Lewis, John Fowles, and Georgette Heyer begin with some variation of "A girl was seen walking …" Sometimes "three young men are seen sitting at a cafe," and some have even been "sighted on a train," but the result is the same: we want to know what they are doing and are willing to stoop to eavesdropping to find out.

Action! 🍃
We arrive on the scene just in time; the story's begun.

The schoolmaster was leaving the village, and everybody seemed sorry. The miller at Cresscombe lent him the small white tilted cart and horse to carry his goods to the city of his destination, about twenty miles off, such a vehicle proving of quite sufficient size for the departing teacher's effects.

—THOMAS HARDY, *Jude the Obscure*

Someone must have been telling lies about Joseph K., for without having done anything wrong he was arrested one fine morning. His landlady's cook, who always brought him his breakfast at eight o'clock, failed to appear on this occasion. That had never happened before.

—FRANZ KAFKA, *The Trial*

The cell door slammed behind Rubashov.

He remained leaning against the door for a few seconds, and lit a cigarette. On the bed to his right lay two fairly clean blankets, and the straw mattress looked newly filled. The wash-basin to his left had no plug, but the tap functioned. The can next to it had been freshly disinfected, it did not smell.

—ARTHUR KOESTLER, *Darkness at Noon,* trans. Daphne Hardy

Reveille was sounded, as always, at 5 A.M.—a hammer pounding on a rail outside camp HQ. The ringing noise came faintly on and off through the windowpanes covered with ice more than an inch thick, and died away fast. It was cold and the warder didn't feel like going on banging.

—ALEXANDER SOLZHENITSYN, *One Day in the Life of Ivan Denisovich,* trans. Max Hayward and Ronald Hingley

The boy with fair hair lowered himself down the last few feet of rock and began to pick his way toward the lagoon. Though he had taken off his school sweater and trailed it now from one hand, his grey shirt stuck to him and his hair was plastered to his forehead. All round him the long scar smashed into the jungle was a bath of heat. He was clambering heavily among the creepers and broken trunks when a bird, a vision of red and yellow, flashed upwards with a witch-like cry; and this cry was echoed by another.

"Hi!" it said. "Wait a minute!"

—WILLIAM GOLDING, *Lord of the Flies*

Thirteen's a Crowd 🦋
We join a group to see what's going on.

Boys are playing basketball around a telephone pole with a backboard bolted to it. Legs, shouts. The scrape and snap of Keds on loose alley pebbles seems to catapult their voices high into the moist March air blue above the wires. Rabbit Angstrom, coming up the alley in a business suit, stops and watches, though he's twenty-six and six three.

—JOHN UPDIKE, *Rabbit, Run*

It was the evening on which MM. Debienne and Poligny, the managers of the Opera, were giving a last gala performance to mark their retirement. Suddenly the dressing-room of La Sorelli, one of the principal dancers, was invaded by half-a-dozen young ladies of the ballet, who had come up from the stage after "dancing" *Polyeucte*. They rushed in amid great confusion, some giving vent to forced and unnatural laughter, others to cries of terror. Sorelli, who wished to be alone for a moment to "run through" the speech which she was to make to the resigning managers, looked around angrily at the mad and tumultuous crowd. It was little Jammes—the girl with the tip-tilted nose, the forget-me-not eyes, the rose-red cheeks and the lily-white neck and shoulders—who gave the explanation in a trembling voice:

"It's the ghost!" And she locked the door.

—GASTON LEROUX, *The Phantom of the Opera*

A surging, seething, murmuring crowd of beings that are human only in name, for to the eye and ear they seem naught but savage creatures, animated by vile passions and by the lust of vengeance and of hate. The hour, some little time before sunset, and the place, the West Barricade, at the very spot where, a decade later, a proud tyrant raised an undying monument to the nation's glory and his own vanity.

During the greater part of the day the guillotine had been kept busy at its ghastly work: all that France had boasted of in the past centuries, of ancient names, and blue blood, had paid toll to her desire for liberty and for fraternity. The carnage had only ceased at this late hour of the day because there were other more interesting sights for the people to witness, a little while before the final closing of the barricades for the night.

—BARONESS ORCZY, *The Scarlet Pimpernel*

The boys, as they talked to the girls from Marcia Blaine School, stood on the far side of their bicycles holding the handlebars, which established a protective fence of bicycle between the sexes, and the impression that at any moment the boys were likely to be away.

The girls could not take off their panama hats because this was not far from the school gates and hatlessness was an offence.

—MURIEL SPARK, *The Prime of Miss Jean Brodie*

A throng of bearded men, in sad-colored garments, and gray, steeple-crowned hats, intermixed with women, some wearing hoods, and others bareheaded, was assembled in front of a wooden edifice, the door of which was heavily timbered with oak, and studded with iron spikes.

The founders of a new colony, whatever Utopia of human virtue and happiness they might originally project, have invariably recognized it among their earliest practical necessities to allot a portion of the virgin soil as a cemetery, and another portion as the site of a prison.

—NATHANIEL HAWTHORNE, *The Scarlet Letter*

A Girl Was Seen Walking ❦
The author begins with the arrival of a stranger.

On an exceptionally hot evening early in July a young man came out of the garret in which he lodged in S. Place and walked slowly, as though in hesitation, towards K. bridge. He had successfully avoided meeting his landlady on the staircase. His garret was under the roof of a high, five-storied house and was more like a cupboard than a room. The landlady who provided him with garret, dinners, and attendance, lived on the floor below, and every time he went out he was obliged to pass her kitchen, the door of which invariably stood open. And each time he passed, the young man had a sick, frightened feeling, which made him scowl and feel ashamed. He was hopelessly in debt to his landlady, and was afraid of meeting her.

—FYODOR DOSTOYEVSKY, *Crime and Punishment,*
trans. Constance Garnett

Late in the afternoon of a chilly day in February, two gentlemen were sitting alone over their wine, in a well-furnished dining parlor, in the town of P_____, in Kentucky. There were no servants present, and the gentlemen, with chairs closely approaching, seemed to be discussing some subject with great earnestness.

—HARRIET BEECHER STOWE, *Uncle Tom's Cabin*

The evening before my departure for Blithedale, I was returning to my bachelor-apartments, after attending the wonderful exhibition of the Veiled Lady, when an elderly-man of rather shabby appearance met me in an obscure part of the street.

"Mr. Coverdale," said he, softly, "can I speak with you a moment?"

—NATHANIEL HAWTHORNE, *The Blithedale Romance*

On an evening in the latter part of May a middle-aged man was walking homeward from Shaston to the village of Marlott, in the adjoining vale of Blakemore or Blackmoor. The pair of legs that carried him were rickety, and there was a bias in his gait which inclined him somewhat to the left of a straight line. He occasionally gave a smart nod, as if in confirmation of some opinion, though he was not thinking of anything in particular. An empty egg-basket was slung upon his arm, the nap of his hat was ruffled, a patch being quite worn away at its brim where his thumb came in taking it off. Presently he was met by an elderly parson astride on a gray mare, who, as he rode, hummed a wandering tune.

'Good night t'ee,' said the man with the basket.

'Good night, Sir John,' said the parson.

—THOMAS HARDY, *Tess of the d'Urbervilles*

An easterly is the most disagreeable wind in Lyme Bay— Lyme Bay being that largest bite from the underside of England's outstretched southwestern leg—and a person of curiosity could at once have deduced several strong probabilities about the pair who began to walk down the quay at Lyme Regis, the small but ancient eponym of the inbite, one incisively sharp and blustery morning in the late March of 1867.

The Cobb has invited what familiarity breeds for at least seven hundred years, and the real Lymers will never see much more to it than a long claw of old gray wall that flexes itself against the sea.

—JOHN FOWLES, *The French Lieutenant's Woman*

The Mayor of Casterbridge

by Thomas Hardy.

Author of "Far from the Madding Crowd", "A Pair of Blue Eyes", &c.

Chapter I.

One evening of late summer, before the present century had reached its middle-age, a young man & woman, the latter carrying a child, were approaching the large village of Weydon-Priors on foot. They were plainly but not ill clad, though the thick hoar of dust which had accumulated on their shoes & clothing from an obviously long journey lent a disadvantageous shabbiness

The first page of the original manuscript of Thomas Hardy's *The Mayor of Casterbridge*. Hardy changed the beginning phrase to "before the nineteenth century had reached one-third of its span. . . ." (*Thomas Hardy Memorial Collection, Dorset County Museum, Dorchester, Dorset*)

On the Road ❧
The story is already in motion—on a ship, in a carriage, in the air.

On they went, singing "Rest Eternal," and whenever they stopped, their feet, the horses, and the gusts of wind seemed to carry on their singing.

Passers-by made way for the procession, counted the wreaths, and crossed themselves. Some joined in out of curiosity and asked: "Who is being buried?"—"Zhivago," they were told.—"Oh, I see. That's what it is."—"It isn't him. It's his wife."—"Well, it comes to the same thing. May her soul rest in peace. It's a fine funeral."

—BORIS PASTERNAK, *Doctor Zhivago,*
trans. Max Hayward and Manya Harari

The two young men—they were of the English public official class—sat in the perfectly appointed railway carriage. The leather straps to the windows were of virgin newness; the mirrors beneath the new luggage racks immaculate as if they had reflected very little; the bulging upholstery in its luxuriant, regulated curves was scarlet and yellow in an intricate, minute dragon pattern, the design of a geometrician in Cologne. The compartment smelt faintly, hygienically of admirable varnish; the train ran as smoothly—Tietjens remembered thinking—as British gilt-edged securities.

—FORD MADOX FORD, *Parade's End*

On Tuesday the freighter steamed through the Straits of Gibraltar and for five days plowed eastward through the Mediterranean, past islands and peninsulas rich in history, so that on Saturday night the steward advised Dr. Cullinane, "If you wish an early sight of the Holy Land you must be up at dawn." The steward was Italian and was reluctant to use the name Israel. For him, good Catholic that he was, it would always be the Holy Land.

—JAMES A. MICHENER, *The Source*

A rather pretty little chaise on springs, such as bachelors, half-pay officers, staff captains, landowners with about a hundred serfs—in short, all such as are spoken of as "gentlemen of the middling sort"—drive about in, rolled in at the gates of the hotel of the provincial town of N. In the chaise sat a gentleman, not handsome but not bad-looking, not too stout and not too thin; it could not be said that he was old, neither could he be described as extremely young. His arrival in the town created no sensation whatever and was not accompanied by anything remarkable.

—NIKOLAI GOGOL, *Dead Souls,* trans. Constance Garnett

Death as a Beginning 🍂
The author uses death as the circumstance that sets the story in motion.

I wake ... the touch of that cold object against my penis awakens me. I did not know that at times one can urinate without knowing it. I keep my eyes closed. The nearest voices cannot be heard: if I opened my eyes, would I hear them? But my eyelids are heavy, they are lead, and there are brass coins on my tongue and iron hammers in my ears and something, something, something like tarnished silver in my breathing; metal, everything is metal; or again, mineral.

—CARLOS FUENTES, *The Death of Artemio Cruz,*
trans. Sam Hileman

It was inevitable: the scent of bitter almonds always reminded him of the fate of unrequited love. Dr. Juvenal Urbino noticed it as soon as he entered the still darkened house where he had hurried on an urgent call to attend a case that for him had lost all urgency many years before. The Antillean refugee Jeremiah de Saint-Amour, disabled war veteran, photographer of children, and his most sympathetic opponent in chess, had escaped the torments of memory with the aromatic fumes of gold cyanide.

—GABRIEL GARCÍA MÁRQUEZ, *Love in the Time of Cholera,*
trans. Edith Grossman

Mrs. Ferrars died on the night of the 16th–17th September—a Thursday. I was sent for at eight o'clock on the morning of Friday the 17th. There was nothing to be done. She had been dead some hours.

—AGATHA CHRISTIE, *The Murder of Roger Ackroyd*

Francis Marion Tarwater's uncle had been dead for only half a day when the boy got too drunk to finish digging his grave and a Negro named Buford Munson, who had come to get a jug filled, had to finish it and drag the body from the breakfast table where it was still sitting and bury it in a decent and Christian way, with the sign of its Saviour at the head of the grave and enough dirt on top to keep the dogs from digging it up. Buford had come along about noon and when he left at sundown, the boy, Tarwater, had never returned from the still.

—FLANNERY O'CONNOR, *The Violent Bear It Away*

8 ✤ THE QUOTATION

novel that begins with dialogue presents us with much the same experience as entering a room in the middle of a conversation. Our perception of what is going on depends on the fragment of conversation that we hear, and from it and the responses that follow, we begin to piece together a story. Once again we are thrust into the middle of the action and of a plot that is already underway. Naturally, the extent of our interest will depend on the quality of what we overhear. Hopefully, the reader will ask, as eight-year-old Antonie does in the first line of Thomas Mann's *Buddenbrooks*, "And—and—what comes next?" "What do you think she'd do if she caught us?" Kipling's young Maisie asks Dick Heldar in *The Light That Failed*, and we want to know what terrible thing the children have done. Through the opening dialogue, we receive our first impression of the speaker, and, if that person is the main character, an indication of his or her voice, intellect, social class, and nature. As long as the opening quotation interests us, it doesn't have to be overly clever, although some authors strive for the unusual; it is difficult to ignore an opening like Rose Macaulay's "Take my camel, dear," in *The Towers of Trebizond*.

Some authors, among them Kingsley Amis, have relied quite extensively on dialogue openings. With great success, because the quotation, which takes advantage of our instinct to eavesdrop, is such a natural way to begin.

"What's That?"
The action has already begun, and we are there.

"Well, Prince, Genoa and Lucca are now no more than private estates of the Bonaparte family. No, I warn you, that if you do not tell me we are at war, if you again allow yourself to palliate all the infamies and atrocities of this Antichrist (upon my word, I believe he is), I don't know you in future, you are no longer my friend, no longer my faithful slave, as you say. There, how do you do, how do you do? I see I'm scaring you, sit down and talk to me."

— COUNT LEO TOLSTOY, *War and Peace*,
trans. Constance Garnett

"Christmas won't be Christmas without any presents," grumbled Jo, lying on the rug.

"It's so dreadful to be poor!" sighed Meg, looking down at her old dress.

"I don't think it's fair for some girls to have plenty of pretty things and other girls nothing at all," added little Amy, with an injured sniff.

"We've got father and mother and each other," said Beth contentedly, from her corner.

—LOUISA MAY ALCOTT, *Little Women*

"What do you think she'd do if she caught us? We oughtn't to have it, you know," said Maisie.

"Beat me, and lock you up in your bedroom," Dick answered, without hesitation. "Have you got the cartridges?"

—RUDYARD KIPLING, *The Light That Failed*

Hi, teach!

Looka *her!* She's a teacher?

Who she?

Is this 304? Are you Mr. Barringer?

No. I'm Miss Barrett.

I'm supposed to have Mr. Barringer.

I'm Miss Barrett.

You the teacher? You so young.

Hey, she's cute! Hey, teach, can I be in your class?

Please don't block the doorway. Please come in.

Good afternoon, Miss Barnet.

Miss Barrett. My name is on the blackboard. Good morning.

—BEL KAUFMAN, *Up the Down Staircase*

"And—and—what comes next?"

"Oh, yes, yes, what the dickens does come next? *C'est la question, ma très chère demoiselle!*"

Frau Consul Buddenbrook shot a glance at her husband and came to the rescue of her little daughter.

—THOMAS MANN, *Buddenbrooks*, trans. H. T. Lowe-Porter

"Yes, of course, if it's fine tomorrow," said Mrs. Ramsay. "But you'll have to be up with the lark," she added.

To her son these words conveyed an extraordinary joy, as if it were settled, the expedition were bound to take place, and the wonder to which he had looked forward, for years and years it seemed, was, after a night's darkness and a day's sail, within touch.

—VIRGINIA WOOLF, *To the Lighthouse*

"Tom!"

No answer.

"Tom!"

No answer.

"What's gone with that boy, I wonder? You Tom!"

—MARK TWAIN, *The Adventures of Tom Sawyer*

"Take my camel, dear," said my aunt Dot, as she climbed down from this animal on her return from High Mass. The camel, a white Arabian Dhalur (single hump) from the famous herd of the Ruola tribe, had been a parting present,

The first page of the original manuscript of Virginia Woolf's *To the Lighthouse*. Woolf made many further word changes, beginning with the first line: "Yes, of course, if it's fine tomorrow." *(Henry W. and Albert A. Berg Collection, The New York Public Library, Astor, Lenox and Tilden Foundations)* its saddle-bags stuffed with low-carat gold and flashy orient gems, from a rich desert tycoon who owned a Levantine hotel near Palmyra. I always thought it to my aunt's credit that, in view of the camel's provenance, she had not named it Zenobia, Longinus, or Aurelian, as lesser women would have done; she had, instead, always called it, in a distant voice, my camel, or the camel.

—ROSE MACAULAY, *The Towers of Trebizond*

9 ❦ THE FLASHBACK

he flashback is the solution to the writer's quandary of how to arrest the reader's attention in some exciting way, and yet tell the story from its beginning. The flashback permits the author to engage the reader at one point in the character's life, and then, by suspending time, to return to a previous point, from which the story proceeds at a more leisurely pace.

Being a recollection, the flashback requires returning to a place, and the novel's beginning then becomes the description of that place. Ernest Hemingway's *A Farewell to Arms*, Truman Capote's *Breakfast at Tiffany's,* and E. L. Doctorow's *Ragtime* all begin by evoking memories of houses. Sometimes the memory is bitter; sometimes sweet and innocent, as, for instance, in Gabriel García Márquez's *One Hundred Years of Solitude*: "Many years later, as he faced the firing squad, Colonel Aureliano Buendía was to remember that distant afternoon when his father took him to discover ice." As an evocation, the flashback has the hazy romantic aura of reverie. Can any beginning surpass the poetry of Daphne du Maurier's "Last night I dreamt I went to Manderley again"? Or the simplicity of Carson McCullers's "It happened that green and crazy summer when Frankie was twelve years old"?

The flashback works because its structure is entirely familiar to us: it is the way we tell stories in our own lives. "Remember the time we found that old love letter in the trunk in the attic?" "Remember the summer that strange girl nearly drowned at the lake?" Recalling the past to the present, we then return to time remembered.

From Time to Time 🦜
The author remembers how it was.

Last night I dreamt I went to Manderley again. It seemed to me I stood by the iron gate leading to the drive, and for a while I could not enter for the way was barred to me. There was a padlock and a chain upon the gate. I called in my dream to the lodge-keeper, and had no answer, and peering closer through the rusted spokes of the gate I saw that the lodge was uninhabited.

—DAPHNE DU MAURIER, *Rebecca*

In the late summer of that year we lived in a house in a village that looked across the river and the plain to the mountains. In the bed of the river there were pebbles and boulders, dry and white in the sun, and the water was clear and swiftly moving and blue in the channels. Troops went by the house and down the road and the dust they raised powdered the leaves of the trees. The trunks of the trees too were dusty and the leaves fell early that year and we saw the troops marching along the road and the dust rising and leaves, stirred by the breeze, falling and the soldiers marching and afterward the road bare and white except for the leaves.

—ERNEST HEMINGWAY, *A Farewell to Arms*

In those days cheap apartments were almost impossible to find in Manhattan, so I had to move to Brooklyn. This was in 1947, and one of the pleasant features of that summer which I so vividly remember was the weather, which was sunny and mild, flower-fragrant, almost as if the days had been arrested in a seemingly perpetual springtime. I was grateful for that if for nothing else, since my youth, I felt, was at its lowest ebb.

—WILLIAM STYRON, *Sophie's Choice*

In 1902 Father built a house at the crest of the Broadview Avenue hill in New Rochelle, New York. It was a three-story brown shingle with dormers, bay windows and a screened porch. Striped awnings shaded the windows. The family took possession of this stout manse on a sunny day in

June and it seemed for some years thereafter that all their days would be warm and fair.

—E. L. DOCTOROW, *Ragtime*

It happened that green and crazy summer when Frankie was twelve years old. This was the summer when for a long time she had not been a member. She belonged to no club and was a member of nothing in the world. Frankie had become an unjoined person who hung around in doorways, and she was afraid.

—CARSON MCCULLERS, *The Member of the Wedding*

It was a queer, sultry summer, the summer they electrocuted the Rosenbergs, and I didn't know what I was doing in New York. I'm stupid about executions. The idea of being electrocuted makes me sick, and that's all there was to read about in the papers—goggle-eyed headlines staring up at me on every street corner and at the fusty, peanut-smelling mouth of every subway. It had nothing to do with me, but I couldn't help wondering what it would be like, being burned alive all along your nerves.

—SYLVIA PLATH, *The Bell Jar*

When I was a small boy at the beginning of the century I remember an old man who wore knee-breeches and worsted stockings, and who used to hobble about the street of our village with the help of a stick. He must have been getting on for eighty in the year 1807, earlier than which date I suppose I can hardly remember him, for I was born in 1802. A few white locks hung about his ears, his shoulders were bent and his knees feeble, but he was still hale, and was much respected in our little world of Paleham. His name was Pontifex.

—SAMUEL BUTLER, *The Way of All Flesh*

Many years later, as he faced the firing squad, Colonel Aureliano Buendía was to remember that distant afternoon when his father took him to discover ice. At that time Macondo was a village of twenty adobe houses, built on the bank of a river of clear water that ran along a bed of polished stones, which were white and enormous, like prehistoric eggs. The world was so recent that many things lacked names, and in order to indicate them it was necessary to point.

—GABRIEL GARCÍA MÁRQUEZ, *One Hundred Years of Solitude,* trans. Gregory Rabassa

I am always drawn back to places where I have lived, the houses and their neighborhoods. For instance, there is a brownstone in the East Seventies where, during the early years of the war, I had my first New York apartment. It was one room crowded with attic furniture, a sofa and fat chairs upholstered in that itchy, particular red velvet that one associates with hot days on a train. The walls were stucco, and a color rather like tobacco-spit. Everywhere, in the bathroom too, there were prints of Roman ruins freckled brown with age. The single window looked out on a fire escape. Even so, my spirits heightened whenever I felt in my pocket the key to this apartment; with all its gloom, it still was a place of my own, the first, and my books were there, and jars of pencils to sharpen, everything I needed, so I felt, to become the writer I wanted to be.

—TRUMAN CAPOTE, *Breakfast at Tiffany's*

10 ❧ THE EPISTLE

ne of the Victorians' favorite devices was the epistle, usually in the form of a letter, but sometimes written as an entry in a journal. In journal form, the epistle served much the same purpose as first-person narration: it made the reader privy to the hero's deepest thoughts and secrets. The hero was less likely to be as revealing in a letter to a second character; that is, unless his whole purpose in "writing" it was to bare his feelings.

Like beginning dialogue, the opening letter or diary entry draws the reader a portrait of the character: his sensitivity or lack of it, his intelligence or stupidity, his stage of maturity, and his state of mind. The "letter to God" at the beginning of Alice Walker's *The Color Purple* is a wonderful example of character drawing without a word of description.

The letter also has a second purpose: it moves the plot.

The plot can be advanced, too, by the use of a "newspaper story" like that at the beginning of Doris Lessing's *The Grass Is Singing,* or even a public proclamation, as in William Styron's *The Confession of Nat Turner.* Used here to begin the book, it provides necessary background information, and is presented as a short preface.

Take an Epistle 🍃
A letter, a diary entry, begins the story.

3 May. Bistritz.—Left Munich at 8:35 P.M., on 1st May, arriving at Vienna early next morning; should have arrived at 6:46, but train was an hour late. Buda-Pesth seems a wonderful place, from the glimpse which I got of it from the train and the little I could walk through the streets. I feared to go very far from the station, as we arrived late and would start as near the correct time as possible.

—BRAM STOKER, *Dracula*

March 16th
A gentleman friend and I were dining at the Ritz last evening and he said that if I took a pencil and a paper and put down all of my thoughts it would make a book. This almost made me smile as what it would really make would be a whole row of encyclopedias. I mean I seem to be thinking practically all of the time. I mean it is my favorite recreation

and sometimes I sit for hours and do not seem to do anything else but think.

—ANITA LOOS, *Gentlemen Prefer Blondes*

(Autumn 1930)
From my window, the deep solemn massive street.
Cellar-shops where the lamps burn all day, under the shadow of top-heavy balconied façades, dirty plaster frontages embossed with scrollwork and heraldic devices. The whole district is like this: street leading into street of houses like shabby monumental safes crammed with the tarnished valuables and second-hand furniture of a bankrupt middle class.

I am a camera with its shutter open, quite passive, recording, not thinking. Recording the man shaving at the window opposite and the woman in the kimono washing her hair. Some day, all this will have to be developed, carefully printed, fixed.

—CHRISTOPHER ISHERWOOD, *Goodbye to Berlin*

progris riport 1 martch 3
Dr. Strauss says I shoud rite down what I think and remembir and evrey thing that happins to me from now on. I dont no why but he says its importint so they will see if they can use me. I hope they use me becaus Miss Kinnian says mabye

they can make me smart. I want to be smart.
My name is Charlie Gordon I werk in Donners bakery
where Mr Donner gives me 11 dollers a week and bred
or cake if I want. I am 32 yeres old and next munth is my
brithday.

—DANIEL KEYES, Flowers for Algernon

You better not never tell nobody but God. It'd kill your mammy.

Dear God,
   I am fourteen years old. ~~Iam~~ I have always been a good
girl. Maybe you can give me a sign letting me know what is
happening to me.
   Last spring after little Lucious come I heard them fussing.
He was pulling on her arm. She say It too soon, Fonso, I
ain't well. Finally he leave her alone. A week go by, he
pulling on her arm again. She say Naw, I ain't gonna. Can't
you see I'm already half dead, an all of these children.

—ALICE WALKER, The Color Purple

One may as well begin with Helen's letters to her sister.

Howards End,
Tuesday.

Dearest Meg,
   *It isn't going to be what we expected. It is old and little, and
altogether delightful—red brick. We can scarcely pack in as it is, and*

*the dear knows what will happen when Paul (younger son) arrives
tomorrow.*

—E. M. FORSTER, *Howards End*

MURDER MYSTERY

By Special Correspondent
Mary Turner, wife of Richard Turner, a
farmer at Ngesi, was found murdered on the
front veranda of their homestead yesterday
morning. The houseboy, who has been
arrested, has confessed to the crime. No
motive has been discovered. It is thought he
was in search of valuables.

—DORIS LESSING, *The Grass Is Singing*

11 ❧ STATEMENT OF PHILOSOPHY

ying beneath the active plot, the characters, and the setting of a novel is the statement that the author wishes to make. Sometimes a universal truth or a personal observation will have suggested the story, and the author sets up the novel by beginning with that thought. "It is a truth universally acknowledged, that a single man in possession of a good fortune must be in want of a wife," writes Jane Austen in *Pride and Prejudice*. And D. H. Lawrence begins *Lady Chatterley's Lover*: "Ours is essentially a tragic age, so we refuse to take it tragically." The author waxes philosophical for a moment before turning to his characters, plot, or setting. Perhaps the most eloquent and memorable example of such a statement is Dickens' brilliant opening paragraph—for it *is* an entire paragraph—to *A Tale of Two Cities:* "It was the best of times, it was the worst of times, it was the age of wisdom, it was the age of foolishness, it was the epoch of belief, it was the epoch of incredulity, it was the season of Light, it was the season of Darkness, it was the spring of hope, it was the winter of despair …" Dickens leads us on through this catalog of antitheses, before telling us that in fact, the time he has in mind is one very much like the present.

Some of the statements presented in this chapter are profound and predictive of the story; others are merely personal observations used as starting points. All make the reader pause for a moment, reflect, and hopefully begin to nod in assent.

The Whole Truth 🦗
The author sets the story with the introduction of a belief.

It is a truth universally acknowledged, that a single man in possession of a good fortune must be in want of a wife.

However little known the feelings or views of such a man may be on his first entering a neighbourhood, this truth is so well fixed in the minds of the surrounding families, that he is considered as the rightful property of someone or other of their daughters.

—JANE AUSTEN, *Pride and Prejudice*

Ours is essentially a tragic age, so we refuse to take it tragically. The cataclysm has happened, we are among the ruins, we start to build up new little habitats, to have new little hopes. It is rather hard work: there is now no smooth road into the future: but we go round, or scramble over the obsta-

Lady Chatterley's Lover
by D H Lawrence

Ours is essentially a tragic age, ~~so we will not take it tragically~~ *but we refuse* ~~altogether~~ emphatically to be tragic about it.

This was Constance Chatterley's position. The war landed her in a ~~badly tragic~~ *dreadful* situation, and she was determined not to make a tragedy out of it.

She married Clifford Chatterley in 1917, when he was home on leave. They had a month of honeymoon, and he went back to France. In 1918 he was very badly wounded, brought home a wreck. She was twenty-three years old.

After two years, he was restored to comparative health. But the lower part of his body was paralysed for ever. He could wheel himself about in a wheeled chair, and he had a little motor attached to a bath chair, so that he could even make ~~their~~ excursions in the grounds at home.

Clifford had suffered so much, that the capacity for suffering had to some extent left him. He remained strange and bright and cheerful, with his ruddy, quite handsome face, and his bright, ~~~~ *haunted* blue eyes. He had so nearly lost life, that what remained to him

The first pages of the first and second versions of D. H. Lawrence's *Lady Chatterley's Lover,* in original mauscript. Lawrence alters and enlarges on his opening philosophic thought, but the

Lady Chatterley's Lover.

by D.H. Lawrence

Chapter I

Ours is essentially a tragic age, so we refuse to take it tragically. The cataclysm has fallen, we've got used to the ruins, and we start to build up new little habitats, new little hopes. If we can't make a road through the obstacles, we go round, or climb over the top. We've got to live, no matter how many skies have fallen. Having tragically wrung our hands, we now proceed to peel the potatoes, or to put on the wireless.

This was Constance Chatterley's position. The war landed her in a very tight situation. But she made up her mind to live and learn.

She married Clifford Chatterley in 1917, when he was home for a month on leave. They had a month's honeymoon. Then he went back to Flanders. To be shipped over to England again, six months later, more or less in bits. Constance, his wife, was then twenty-three years old, and he was twenty nine.

His hold on life was marvellous. He didn't die, and the bits seemed to grow together again. For two years, he remained in the doctors' hands. Then he was pronounced a cure, and could return to life again, with the lower half of his body, from the hips down, paralysed for ever.

beginning phrase remains firm. (*Harry Ransom Humanities Research Center, The University of Texas at Austin*) cles. We've got to live, no matter how many skies have fallen.

    This was more or less Constance Chatterley's position.
The war had brought the roof down over her head. And she
had realised that one must live and learn.

—D. H. LAWRENCE, *Lady Chatterley's Lover*

It was the best of times, it was the worst of times, it was the
age of wisdom, it was the age of foolishness, it was the epoch
of belief, it was the epoch of incredulity, it was the season of
Light, it was the season of Darkness, it was the spring of
hope, it was the winter of despair, we had everything before
us, we had nothing before us, we were all going direct to
Heaven, we were all going direct the other way—in short,
the period was so far like the present period, that some of its
noisiest authorities insisted on its being received, for good or
for evil, in the superlative degree of comparison only.

—CHARLES DICKENS, *A Tale of Two Cities*

Happy families are all alike; every unhappy family is unhappy
in its own way.

    Everything was in confusion in the Oblonskys' house. The
wife had discovered that the husband was carrying on an
intrigue with a French girl, who had been a governess in
their family, and she had announced to her husband that she
could not go on living in the same house with him.

—COUNT LEO TOLSTOY, *Anna Karenina,*
trans. Constance Garnett

"All happy families are more or less dissimilar; all unhappy ones are more or less alike," says a great Russian writer in the beginning of a famous novel (*Anna Arkadievitch Karenina,* transfigured into English by R. G. Stonelower, Mount Tabor Ltd., 1880). That pronouncement has little if any relation to the story to be unfolded now, a family chronicle, the first part of which is, perhaps, closer to another Tolstoy work, *Detstvo i Otrochestvo (Childhood and Fatherland,* Pontius Press, 1858).

—VLADIMIR NABOKOV, *Ada or Ardor: A Family Chronicle*

A destiny that leads the English to the Dutch is strange enough; but one that leads from Epsom into Pennsylvania, and thence into the hills that shut in Altamont over the proud coral cry of the cock, and the soft stone smile of an angel, is touched by that dark miracle of chance which makes new magic in a dusty world.

Each of us is all the sums he has not counted: subtract us into nakedness and night again, and you shall see begin in Crete four thousand years ago the love that ended yesterday in Texas.

—THOMAS WOLFE, *Look Homeward, Angel*

Time is not a line but a dimension, like the dimensions of space. If you can bend space you can bend time also, and if you knew enough and could move faster than light you could travel backward in time and exist in two places at once.

—MARGARET ATWOOD, *Cat's Eye*

12 &A LITTLE BACKGROUND

ometimes as an author begins to tell a story, he realizes that in order for the reader to fully understand what he is about to relate, a certain amount of background is necessary. It may be a description of a place or an era, or the past history of a character, but its purpose is more than description, it is explanation. It gives us the information we need to knowledgeably begin the story at the point the novelist has chosen. "In the time of Spanish rule, and for many years afterwards, the town of Sulaco—the luxuriant beauty of the orange gardens bears witness to its antiquity—had never been commercially anything more important than a coasting port with a fairly large local trade in ox-hides and indigo," sets up Joseph Conrad's *Nostromo.*

A short backgrounding paragraph at the beginning of a novel is a part of the novel proper: it starts the story. However, when the backgrounding information is so extensive that it threatens to stall the story, it is often allotted to a preface. As we will see in a later chapter, the backgrounding preface is usually unconnected to the action: the story must wait.

Back Up, Please ❦
First we're given some history.

August, 1931—The port town of Veracruz is a little purgatory between land and sea for the traveler, but the people who live there are very fond of themselves and the town they have helped to make. They live as initiates in local custom reflecting their own history and temperament, and they carry on their lives of alternate violence and lethargy with a pleasurable contempt for outside opinion, founded on the charmed notion that their ways and feelings are above and beyond criticism.

—KATHERINE ANNE PORTER, *Ship of Fools*

In that pleasant district of merry England which is watered by the river Don, there extended in ancient times a large forest, covering the greater part of the beautiful hills and valleys which lie between Sheffield and the pleasant town of Doncaster. The remains of this extensive wood are still to be seen at the noble seats of Wentworth, of Wharncliffe Park, and around Rotherham. Here haunted of yore the fabulous Dragon of Wantley; here were fought many of the most desperate battles during the civil Wars of the Roses; and here also flourished in ancient times those bands of gallant outlaws whose deeds have been rendered so popular in English song.

—SIR WALTER SCOTT, *Ivanhoe*

St. Botolphs was an old place, an old river town. It had been an inland port in the great days of the Massachusetts sailing fleets and now it was left with a factory that manufactured table silver and a few other small industries. The natives did not consider that it had diminished much in size or importance, but the long roster of the Civil War dead, bolted to the cannon on the green, was a reminder of how populous the village had been in the 1860's.

—JOHN CHEEVER, *The Wapshot Chronicle*

In the days when the spinning wheels hummed busily in the farmhouses—and even great ladies, clothed in silk and thread-lace, had their toy spinning wheels of polished oak—there might be seen, in districts far away among the lanes, or deep in the bosom of the hills, certain pallid undersized men who, by the side of the brawny countryfolk, looked like the remnants of a disinherited race. The shepherd's dog barked fiercely when one of these alien-looking men appeared on the upland, dark against the early winter sunset; for what dog likes a figure bent under a heavy bag?—and these pale men rarely stirred abroad without that mysterious burden.

—GEORGE ELIOT, *Silas Marner*

They used to hang men at Four Turnings in the old days.

Not any more, though. Now, when a murderer pays the penalty for his crime, he does so up at Bodmin, after fair trial at the Assizes. That is, if the law convicts him before his own conscience kills him. It is better so. Like a surgical operation. And the body has decent burial, though a nameless grave.

—DAPHNE DU MAURIER, *My Cousin Rachel*

The Prince had always liked his London, when it had come to him; he was one of the modern Romans who find by the Thames a more convincing image of the truth of the ancient state than any they have left by the Tiber. Brought up on the legend of the City to which the world paid tribute, he recognized in the present London much more than in contemporary Rome the real dimensions of such a case. If it was a question of an *Imperium,* he said to himself, and if one wished, as a Roman, to recover a little the sense of that, the place to do so was on London Bridge, or even, on a fine afternoon in May, at Hyde Park Corner.

—HENRY JAMES, *The Golden Bowl*

The Browns have become illustrious by the pen of Thackeray and the pencil of Doyle, within the memory of the young gentlemen who are now matriculating at the Universities. Notwithstanding the well-merited but late fame which has now fallen upon them, any one at all acquainted with the family must feel, that much has yet to be written and said

The first page of the original manuscript of J. M. Barrie's *The Little Minister*. In the final version, the opening line was changed to: "Long ago in the days when our caged blackbirds never saw a king's soldier without whistling impudently. . . . " *(Henry W. and Albert A. Berg Collection, The New York Public Library, Astor, Lenox and Tilden Foundations)* before the British nation will be properly sensible of how much of its greatness it owes to the Browns. For centuries, in their quiet, dogged, homespun way, they have been subduing the earth in most English counties, and leaving their mark in American forests and Australian uplands. Wherever the fleets and armies of England have won renown, there stalwart sons of the Browns have done yeomen's work.

—AN OLD BOY [Thomas Hughes], *Tom Brown's School Days*

The family of Dashwood had been long settled in Sussex. Their estate was large, and their residence was at Norland Park, in the centre of their property, where, for many generations, they had lived in so respectable a manner, as to engage the general good opinion of their surrounding acquaintance.

—JANE AUSTEN, *Sense and Sensibility*

Major Amberson had "made a fortune" in 1873, when other people were losing fortunes, and the magnificence of the Ambersons began then. Magnificence, like the size of a fortune, is always comparative, as even Magnificent Lorenzo may now perceive, if he has happened to haunt New York in 1916; and the Ambersons were magnificent in their day and place. Their splendour lasted throughout all the years that saw their Midland town spread and darken into a city, but reached its topmost during the period when every prosperous family with children kept a Newfoundland dog.

—BOOTH TARKINGTON, *The Magnificent Ambersons*

13 ❧ The Preface

he type of preface included in this chapter is not the non-fictional, personal author's note that is meant to give the reader some insight into the writing of the novel, but the preface that is an integral part of the story. Called a preface, an introduction, a prologue or a foreword, it contributes importantly to the novel, providing the framework within which the story can be told.

As we have noted, the preface can supply the reader with the background necessary to understand the plot or the characters without slowing down the story; Chapter 1 begins as if the preface did not exist. A good example of this kind of preface is Stevenson's Introductory to *Weir of Hermiston*. The preface can also set up a flashback, beginning with an episode of the novel, and returning in the first chapter to a previous time. So Charles Ryder, camped with C Company on the grounds of the Brideshead estate in the Prologue of Evelyn Waugh's

Brideshead Revisited, is reminded of his life with Sebastian and Julia, and can begin to tell their story in Chapter 1.

In some cases the preface takes the form of the faux-author's note. The preface sets up the narrator as the finder of a manuscript of memoirs, a journal, or a book, which he then begins to reveal—as written—beginning with the first chapter, as in L. P. Hartley's *The Go-Between.* Or it details the circumstances under which the "writer" was persuaded or moved to tell the story that is to follow, in his own words, as in W. H. Hudson's *Green Mansions* or Giorgio Bassani's *The Garden of the Finzi-Continis.*

What should be becoming obvious is that the preface and its subsequent first chapter can begin with any combination of the techniques we have been examining. In fact, the preface is an ingenious solution to the problem of where to start, particularly if the writer is enamored of two "perfect" openings: with the preface, he can have them both. The preface can begin with Background, and the first chapter with the Entrance of the Hero; it can start with Something Happening and Flash Back to a Setting; it can lead with a note from the Author and be followed by a First Person narrative. The combinations are, happily, endless.

The Faux-Author Preface 🦋
The "author" explains the source of the story he is about to tell.

This book contains the records left us by a man whom, according to the expression he often used himself, we called the Steppenwolf. Whether this manuscript needs any introductory remarks may be open to question. I, however, feel the need of adding a few pages to those of the Steppenwolf in which I try to record my recollections of him.

       —HERMANN HESSE, Preface, *Steppenwolf,*
       trans. Basil Creighton

The day had gone by just as days go by. I had killed it in accordance with my primitive and retiring way of life.

       —Harry Haller's Records, *Steppenwolf*

The past is a foreign country: they do things differently there.
    When I came upon the diary it was lying at the bottom of a rather battered red cardboard collar-box, in which as a small boy I kept my Eton collars. Someone, probably my mother, had filled it with treasures dating from those days.

       —L. P. HARTLEY, Prologue, *The Go-Between*

The eighth of July was a Sunday and on the following Monday I left West Hatch, the village where we lived near Salisbury, for Brandham Hall. My mother arranged that my Aunt Charlotte, a Londoner, should take me across London. Between bouts of stomach-turning trepidation I looked forward wildly to the visit.

       —Chapter 1, *The Go-Between*

For many years I wanted to write about the Finzi-Continis—about Micòl and Alberto, about Professor Ermanno and Signora Olga—and about all the others who inhabited or, like me, frequented the house in Corso Ercole I d'Este, in Ferrara, just before the outbreak of the last war. But the stimulus, the impulse to do it really came to me only a year ago, on a Sunday in April 1957.

> —GIORGIO BASSANI, Prologue, *The Garden of the Finzi-Continis,* trans. William Weaver

The tomb was big, massive, really imposing: a kind of half-ancient, half-Oriental temple of the sort seen in the sets of *Aïda* and *Nabucco* in vogue in our opera houses until a few years ago.

> —Part I, *The Garden of the Finzi-Continis*

About a year ago, when I was in the royal library doing research for my history of Louis XIV, I happened to come upon the *Memoirs of Monsieur d'Artagnan,* which, like most works of that time, when authors wanted to tell the truth without having to spend time in the Bastille, was printed in Amsterdam, by Pierre Rouge. The title attracted me; I took the book home, with the librarian's permission, of course, and devoured it.

> —ALEXANDRE DUMAS, Preface, *The Three Musketeers*

On the first Monday of April, 1625, the market town of Meung, birthplace of the author of the *Roman de la Rose,* seemed to be in as great a turmoil as if the Huguenots had come to turn it into a second La Rochelle. A number of townsmen, seeing women running in the direction of the main street and hearing children shouting on doorsteps, hastened to put on their breastplates and, steadying their rather uncertain self-assurance with a musket or a halberd, made their way toward the inn, the Hôtellerie du Franc Meunier, in front of which a noisy, dense, and curious throng was growing larger by the minute.

—Chapter 1, *The Three Musketeers*

It is a cause of very great regret to me that this task has taken so much longer a time than I had expected for its completion. It is now many months—over a year, in fact—since I wrote to Georgetown announcing my intention of publishing, *in a very few months,* the whole truth about Mr. Abel.

—W. H. HUDSON, Prologue, *Green Mansions*

Now that we are cool, he said, and regret that we hurt each other, I am not sorry that it happened. I deserved your reproach: a hundred times I have wished to tell you the whole story of my travels and adventures among the savages, and one of the reasons which prevented me was the fear that it would have an unfortunate effect on our friendship.

—Chapter 1, *Green Mansions*

The writer, an old man with a white moustache, had some difficulty in getting into bed. The windows of the house in which he lived were high and he wanted to look at the trees when he awoke in the morning. A carpenter came to fix the bed so that it would be on a level with the window.
—Sherwood Anderson, The Book of the Grotesque,
Winesburg, Ohio

Upon the half decayed veranda of a small frame house that stood near the edge of a ravine near the town of Winesburg, Ohio, a fat little old man walked nervously up and down.
—Chapter 1, *Winesburg, Ohio*

More Prefaces 🦋
A variety of openings.

I am an invisible man. No, I am not a spook like those who haunted Edgar Allan Poe; nor am I one of your Hollywood-movie ectoplasms. I am a man of substance, of flesh and bone, fiber and liquids—and I might even be said to possess a mind. I am invisible, understand, simply because people refuse to see me.
—Ralph Ellison, Prologue, *Invisible Man*

It goes a long way back, some twenty years. All my life I had been looking for something, and everywhere I turned some-one tried to tell me what it was. I accepted their answers too, though they were often in contradiction and even self-contra-

dictory. I was naïve. I was looking for myself and asking everyone except myself questions which I, and only I, could answer.
—Chapter 1, *Invisible Man*

When I reached C Company lines, which were at the top of
the hill, I paused and looked back at the camp, just coming
into full view below me through the grey mist of early
morning. We were leaving that day. When we marched in,
three months before, the place was under snow; now the first
leaves of spring were unfolding. I had reflected then that,
whatever scenes of desolation lay ahead of us, I never feared
one more brutal than this, and I reflected now that it had no
single happy memory for me.
—EVELYN WAUGH, Prologue, *Brideshead Revisited*

"I have been here before," I said; I had been there before;
first with Sebastian more than twenty years ago on a cloud-
less day in June, when the ditches were creamy with mead-
owsweet and the air heavy with all the scents of summer; it
was a day of peculiar splendour, and though I had been there
so often, in so many moods, it was to that first visit that my
heart returned on this, my latest.
—Book One, *Brideshead Revisited*

One summer evening in the year 1848, three Cardinals and a
missionary Bishop from America were dining together in the

gardens of a villa in the Sabine hills, overlooking Rome. The villa was famous for the fine view from its terrace. The hidden garden in which the four men sat at table lay some twenty feet below the south end of this terrace, and was a mere shelf of rock, overhanging a steep declivity planted with vineyards.

—WILLA CATHER, Prologue: At Rome,
Death Comes for the Archbishop

One afternoon in the autumn of 1851 a solitary horseman, followed by a pack-mule, was pushing through an arid stretch of country somewhere in central New Mexico. He had lost his way, and was trying to get back to the trail, with only his compass and his sense of direction for guides.

—Book One, *Death Comes for the Archbishop*

The artist is the creator of beautiful things.
   To reveal art and conceal the artist is art's aim.
The critic is he who can translate into another manner or a new material his impression of beautiful things.
   The highest as the lowest form of criticism is a mode of
   autobiography.
Those who find ugly meanings in beautiful things are corrupt without being charming. This is a fault.
      Those who find beautiful meanings in beautiful
      things are the cultivated. For these there is hope....

—OSCAR WILDE, The Preface, *The Picture of Dorian Gray*

The studio was filled with the rich odour of roses, and when the light summer wind stirred amidst the trees of the garden there came through the open door the heavy scent of the lilac, or the more delicate perfume of the pink-flowering thorn.

—Chapter 1, *The Picture of Dorian Gray*

Who that cares much to know the history of man, and how the mysterious mixture behaves under the varying experiments of Time, has not dwelt, at least briefly, on the life of Saint Theresa, has not smiled with some gentleness at the thought of the little girl walking forth one morning hand in hand with her still smaller brother to go and seek martyrdom in the country of the Moors?

—GEORGE ELIOT, Prelude, *Middlemarch*

Miss Brooke had that kind of beauty which seems to be thrown into relief by poor dress. Her hand and wrist were so finely formed that she could wear sleeves not less bare of style than those in which the blessed Virgin appeared to Italian painters; and her profile as well as her stature and bearing seemed to gain the more dignity from her plain garments, which by the side of provincial fashion gave her the impressiveness of a fine quotation from the Bible—or from one of our elder poets—in a paragraph of today's newspaper.

—Chapter 1, *Middlemarch*

*We are talking now of summer evenings in Knoxville, Tennessee, in
the time that I lived there so successfully disguised to myself as a
child. It was a little bit mixed sort of block, fairly solidly lower middle class, with one or two juts apiece on either side of that.*
                              —JAMES AGEE, Knoxville: Summer, 1915*,
                                        A Death in the Family

At supper that night, as many times before, his father said,
"Well, spose we go to the picture show."

"Oh, Jay!" his mother said. "That horrid little man!"

"What's wrong with him?" his father asked, not because
he didn't know what she would say, but so she would say it.

"He's so *nasty!*" she said, as she always did. "So *vulgar!*
With his nasty little cane; hooking up skirts and things, and
that nasty little walk!"

                              —Chapter 1, *A Death in the Family*

*Presented as a preface in the posthumous printing of the book on the
premise that the editors would have urged him to do so.

14 🐝 BREVITY COUNTS

he dramatically short sentence seems such a modern technique that it comes as something of a revelation to open *Bleak House* and read: "London. Michaelmas Term lately over, and the Lord Chancellor sitting in Lincoln's Inn Hall. Implacable November weather." But then, Dickens was endlessly inventive. It is almost more unusual to find an Edwardian, like Hugh Walpole, so enamored with the brief, declarative sentence that he used it again and again. "Robin Trojan was waiting for his father," begins *The Wooden Horse*; "Young Cole, quivering with pride, surveyed the room," *Jeremy at Crale*; and "The fog had swallowed up the house, and the house had submitted," *The Green Mirror*.

The three- or four-word sentence gives a novel a fast start. It sets a pace and a rhythm. And it has all the impact of understatement. "Mother died today," begins Albert Camus's

The Stranger, and we are shocked, both by the abruptness of the disclosure and by the narrator's matter-of-factness. "They're out there," opens Ken Kesey's *One Flew Over the Cuckoo's Nest,* and three carefully-chosen words reveal all the narrator's paranoia. "Nobody could sleep," writes Norman Mailer in *The Naked and the Dead,* and we feel the quiet panic of troops facing the unknowable.

Perhaps more than any other technique, the short first sentence must be *exactly* right. Like a line of poetry—and each of the first lines quoted above easily could be the start of a poem—every single word counts, and the combination of those few carefully chosen words is extremely powerful. For the novelist troubled by the wordiness of a beginning description of setting or character, three little words might say it all.

Short and Sweet 🍀
The well-chosen word or two.

I was born. It was born. So it began. It continues. It will outlive me. People whisper, stare, giggle. Their eternal privilege. My eternal curse.

—JOYCE CAROL OATES, *The Assassins*

London. Michaelmas Term lately over, and the Lord Chancellor sitting in Lincoln's Inn Hall. Implacable November weather. As much mud in the streets, as if the waters had but newly retired from the face of the earth, and it would not be wonderful to meet a Megalosaurus, forty feet long or so, waddling like an elephantine lizard up Holborn Hill.

—CHARLES DICKENS, *Bleak House*

Mother died today. Or, maybe, yesterday; I can't be sure. The telegram from the Home says: YOUR MOTHER PASSED AWAY. FUNERAL TOMORROW. DEEP SYM-PATHY. Which leaves the matter doubtful; it could have been yesterday.

—ALBERT CAMUS, *The Stranger,* trans. Stuart Gilbert

It was Wang Lung's marriage day. At first, opening his eyes in the blackness of the curtains about his bed, he could not think why the dawn seemed different from any other.

—PEARL S. BUCK, *The Good Earth*

They're out there.

Black boys in white suits up before me to commit sex acts in the hall and get it mopped up before I can catch them.

They're mopping when I come out the dorm, all three of them sulky and hating everything, the time of day, the place they're at here, the people they got to work around. When they hate like this, better if they don't see me.

—KEN KESEY, *One Flew Over the Cuckoo's Nest*

Dusk—of a summer night.

And the tall walls of the commercial heart of an American city of perhaps 400,000 inhabitants—such walls as in time may linger as a mere fable.

—THEODORE DREISER, *An American Tragedy*

124 was spiteful. Full of a baby's venom. The women in the house knew it and so did the children. For years each put up with the spite in his own way, but by 1873 Sethe and her daughter Denver were its only victims.

—TONI MORRISON, *Beloved*

Nobody could sleep. When morning came, assault craft would be lowered and a first wave of troops would ride through the surf and charge ashore on the beach at Anopopei. All over the ship, all through the convoy, there was a knowledge that in a few hours some of them were going to be dead.

—NORMAN MAILER, *The Naked and the Dead*

It was love at first sight.

The first time Yossarian saw the chaplain he fell madly in love with him.

Yossarian was in the hospital with a pain in his liver that fell just short of being jaundice. The doctors were puzzled by the fact that it wasn't quite jaundice. If it became jaundice they could treat it. If it didn't become jaundice and went away they could discharge him. But this just being short of jaundice all the time confused them.

—JOSEPH HELLER, *Catch-22*

Howard Roark laughed.

He stood naked at the edge of a cliff. The lake lay far below him. A frozen explosion of granite burst in flight to the sky over motionless water. The water seemed immovable, the stone—flowing. The stone had the stillness of one brief moment in battle when thrust meets thrust and the currents are held in a pause more dynamic than motion. The stone glowed, wet with sunrays.

—AYN RAND, *The Fountainhead*

I am ill; I am full of spleen and repellent. I conceive there to be something wrong with my liver, for I cannot even think for the aching of my head. Yet what my complaint is I do not know. Medicine I cannot, I never could, take, although for medicine and doctors I have much reverence. Also, I am extremely superstitious: which, it may be, is why I cherish such a respect for the medical profession. I am well-educated, and therefore might have risen superior to such fancies, yet of them I am full to the core.

—FYODOR DOSTOYEVSKY, *Letters from the Underworld,*
trans. C. J. Hogarth

543 1. 1.
Catch-22
3395

I
THE TEXAN) see cover

It was love at first sight.

The first time Yossarian saw the chaplain he fell madly in love with him.

Yossarian)

~~He~~ was in the hospital, ~~~~~~~~~~~~~~ with a pain in his liver that fell just short of being jaundice. The doctors were puzzled by the fact that it wasn't quite jaundice. If it became jaundice they could treat it. If it didn't become jaundice and went away they could discharge him. But this just being short of jaundice all the time ~~only~~ confused them.

Each morning they came around, three brisk and serious men with efficient mouths and inefficient eyes, accompanied by brisk and serious Nurse Duckett, one of the ward nurses who didn't like Yossarian. They read the chart at the foot of the bed and ~~then~~ asked impatiently about the pain. They seemed irritated when he told them it was exactly the same.

"Still no movement?" the full colonel demanded.

The doctors exchanged a look when he shook his head.

"Give him another pill."

First page of the original manuscript of Joseph Heller's *Catch-22*. *(Joseph Heller Collection, Brandeis University Library, Special Collections Department)*

A squat grey building of only thirty-four stories. Over the main entrance the words, CENTRAL LONDON HATCHERY AND CONDITIONING CENTRE, and, in a shield, the World State's motto, COMMUNITY, IDENTITY, STABILITY.

—ALDOUS HUXLEY, *Brave New World*

15 &❧ BREVITY DOESN'T COUNT

. E. Lawrence, acknowledging in an author's note to his *Seven Pillars of Wisdom* the many "suggestions" Charlotte and Bernard Shaw had made in regards to his masterpiece (Shaw had actually edited the book at Lawrence's request), also thanked them for "all the present semicolons." Shaw's writing is a study in the proper use of the semicolon, and, despite H. G. Wells's attempts to introduce him to the dash, he never abandoned it. Both the semicolon and the dash, of course, allow the writer to combine two or more independent thoughts that could otherwise have stood on their own as shorter sentences. They give a sentence enhanced emphasis, especially if the second part contradicts the first. They also sometimes give it a breathtaking length.

Although Henry James immediately comes to mind when we think about 100+-word sentences, he was certainly not alone in his longwindedness. (Did people speak then as they wrote?) The Victorian and Edwardian novel abounds in labyrinthian sentences that might more properly be called paragraphs. However, prodigious length did not necessarily presume dullness. The beginning sentence-paragraph of Jane Austen's *Persuasion,* with its multiple sprinkling of semi-colons, is as witty as it is astute, and requires no effort of concentration at all to follow its connected clauses.

Time and stylistic changes have altered the carefully con-structed, logically sequenced Victorian sentence to a twenti-eth-century version that is free-form and almost stream of consciousness. A sentence like Joyce Carol Oates's 213-word opening to *Bellefleur does* require more concentration, but if we stay with it, by the end of the paragraph we are left with a good feeling for the book's rhythm and tone, and an initial insight into the characters.

One Hundred and Counting 🐓
The 100+-word sentence.

The young man walks fast by himself through the crowd that thins into the night streets; feet are tired from hours of walk-ing; eyes greedy for warm curve of faces, answering flicker of eyes, the set of a head, the lift of a shoulder, the way hands spread and clench; blood tingles with wants; mind is a bee-hive of hopes buzzing and stinging; muscles ache for the knowledge of jobs, for the roadmender's pick and shovel work, the fisherman's knack with a hook when he hauls on

the slithery net from the rail of the lurching trawler, the
swing of the bridgeman's arm as he slings down the whitehot
rivet, the engineer's slow grip wise on the throttle, the dirt-
farmer's use of his whole body when, whoaing the mules, he
yanks the plow from the furrow. The young man walks by
himself searching through the crowd with greedy eyes,
greedy ears taut to hear, by himself, alone.

—JOHN DOS PASSOS, *U.S.A.*

It was many years ago in that dark, chaotic, unfathomable
pool of time before Germaine's birth (nearly twelve months
before her birth), on a night in late September stirred by
innumerable frenzied winds, like spirits contending with one
another—now plaintively, now angrily, now with a subtle
cellolike delicacy capable of making the flesh rise on one's
arms and neck—a night so sulfurous, so restless, so swollen
with inarticulate longing that Leah and Gideon Bellefleur in
their enormous bed quarreled once again, brought to tears
because their love was too ravenous to be contained by their
mere mortal bodies; and their groping, careless, anguished
words were like strips of raw silk rubbed violently together
(for each was convinced that the other did not, *could* not, be
equal to his love—Leah doubted that any man was capable of
a love so profound it could lie silent, like a forest pond;
Gideon doubted that any woman was capable of compre-
hending the nature of a man's passion, which might tear
through him, rendering him broken and exhausted, as vulnerable as a small child): it was on this tumultuous rain-

lashed night that Mahalaleel came to Bellefleur Manor on the western shore of the great Lake Noir, where he was to stay for nearly five years.

—JOYCE CAROL OATES, *Bellefleur*

Among other public buildings in a certain town, which for many reasons it will be prudent to refrain from mentioning, and to which I will assign no fictitious name, there is one anciently common to most towns, great or small: to wit, a workhouse; and in this workhouse was born; on a day and date which I need not trouble myself to repeat, inasmuch as it can be of no possible consequence to the reader, in this stage of the business at all events; the item of mortality whose name is prefixed to the head of this chapter.

—CHARLES DICKENS, *Oliver Twist*

I, Tiberius Claudius Drusus Nero Germanicus This-that-and-the-other (for I shall not trouble you yet with all my titles) who was once, and not so long ago either, known to my friends and relatives and associates as "Claudius the Idiot," or "That Claudius," or "Claudius the Stammerer," or "Clau-Clau-Claudius" or at best as "Poor Uncle Claudius," am now about to write this strange history of my life; starting from my earliest childhood and continuing year by year until I reach the fateful point of change where, some eight years ago, at the age of fifty-one, I suddenly found myself caught in what I may call the "golden predicament" from which I have never since become disentangled.

—ROBERT GRAVES, *I, Claudius*

Sir Walter Elliot, of Kellynch Hall, in Somersetshire, was a man who, for his own amusement, never took up any book but the Baronetage; there he found occupation for an idle hour, and consolation in a distressed one; there his faculties were roused into admiration and respect by contemplating the limited remnant of the earliest patents; there any unwelcome sensations arising from domestic affairs changed naturally into pity and contempt as he turned over the almost endless creations of the last century; and there, if every other leaf were powerless, he could read his own history with an interest which never failed.

—JANE AUSTEN, *Persuasion*

16 ❧ THE END

Any serious writer would consider him or herself blessed to have composed even a single opening line from some of the selections in this book. That many authors were able to repeat this miracle in book after book, and then build upon those first lines to create stories and characters that live for us long after we have finished reading—some for the rest of our lives—is daunting enough to keep us from pen and paper forever. The joy of writing, however, is that there is no "right" way to write, no "right" style to use, no "right" way to begin. Ten novelists describing a mountain would describe ten different mountains. If nothing else, *Great Beginnings and Endings* is comforting proof of the fact that every writer's voice is unique, and it is the differences, not the similarities, that make a story worth beginning.

Great Beginnings. Short. Long. Descriptive. Active. Philosophic. Each of them a small gem, a mini-masterpiece, and most of all, a joyful solution to Bertie Wooster's "dashed difficult problem of where to begin."

. . . AND ENDINGS

17 ❧ INTRODUCTION

A few years ago, there appeared on Broadway a musical with a rather unusual premise: it had no ending. More correctly, it had multiple endings. Because at the conclusion of Act II the audience was invited to choose which of the major characters before them on stage had committed the murder around which the plot revolved.

The musical was *The Mystery of Edwin Drood*, based on Charles Dickens's last novel, and the unique non-ending was necessary because the book itself has no ending; the author had not finished it at the time of his death. Although Dickens left many clues, and his own daughter supported the theory that the murderer was Drood's uncle, John Jasper, Dickens scholars can be no more certain of this solution to the mystery than the Broadway audiences, who often made other choices.

The evening I saw the performance, the audience, which had been restlessly struggling to hear and understand the show's intricate lyrics, became instantly alert as it was offered the opportunity of deciding the ending. And although the "voting" was all in fun, it nevertheless gave the audience a small taste of the responsibility every novelist faces as he or she draws near the last pages of a book: how to end?

Happy or unhappy, hopeful or devastating, the ending brings the story to what is, for the author, the inevitable conclusion. In some respects, ending a story is probably easier than beginning it; conceivably the characters have taken on lives of their own and suggested their own destinies. But ultimately, it is the author who must liberate or kill them, separate or marry them, destroy or save them. And while the author must be true to the characters, he or she must consider the reader as well. For, if a great beginning is vital in capturing a reader's interest, a great ending is equally important in not letting a reader down.

Just as there are many possible ways to begin a story, there are countless ways to end it. In the nascent years of the modern novel, the reader's natural desire for a story to conclude happily for the hero or heroine traditionally led to the type of ending we find in the Austen novels: a marriage, blessed with property and good fortune. In the Victorian and the Edwardian periods, when most novels appeared first in magazine serialization, the importance of satisfying the magazine reader's desire for a happy outcome often resulted in stories with two endings, with the subsequently published book containing the author's preferred, often unhappy, version.

No matter what the outcome, however, the last page of a novel is where loose ends must be tied. In Jane Austen's time, this meant accounting for the future lives of all the major characters in a summary paragraph. In many novels, the last paragraph returns to the opening, like the completion of a circle, echoing the theme, even the title, of the book. Still others paint a last portrait of the hero or heroine having faced the fulfillment or the destruction of his or her life and greeting the future with a new sense of hope. Some endings are so extraordinary that the last lines remain in our memory, like poetry. Consider for instance, *Gone With the Wind*: "I'll think of it all tomorrow, at Tara. I can stand it then. Tomorrow, I'll think of some way to get him back. After all, tomorrow is another day." A popular movie and years of parody have made these lines famous, but the desperately brave words of the indomitable Scarlett O'Hara still haunt us from the last page of Margaret Mitchell's classic. They do more than end the story—they leave us satisfied and filled with hope.

This section contains a collection of memorable ending lines from great novels, again dating from the time of Jane Austen, and including selections from much of the world's finest literature, enabling us to examine, compare, and learn from the choices great authors have made. Since it is inevitable that a novelist who began a book brilliantly would end it equally brilliantly, many of the books begun in the first half of this book will be found ending in this part. There are many new entries, however, chosen from an endlessly rich variety, including works written both in English and in other languages.

One difference between beginnings and endings that immediately comes to mind, of course, is that while a reader needs no previous information to understand a beginning, an ending assumes a good deal of foreknowledge about a novel's characters, plot, and setting. However, I believe that to summarize what has gone before in each novel would have lessened the impact of the bare words and so, in most cases, the passage has been allowed to speak for itself, to be enjoyed and admired as the fine writing it is. Still, where an ending would be totally incomprehensible standing alone, I have prefaced it with a short note.

In the end, it is the novelists who have the last word.

18 ❧ HAPPILY EVER AFTER

t is human nature to yearn for happiness. And inevitably our love affair with romance has created generations of disillusioned men and women who were led to believe that marriage was automatically followed by "and they lived happily ever after." Isn't that what always happens in novels?

Reading Jane Austen's *Pride and Prejudice*, we trust from the start that it is only a matter of time before Darcy and Elizabeth find their way to the altar. And a still shorter time before the one obstacle to their happiness, the disapproval of Darcy's aunt, Lady Catherine, is conquered by Elizabeth's patient good nature. All of Jane Austen's novels inevitably end with a marriage or two, "true love, and no want of fortune and friends," and with all of these advantages, it is an understatement to say, as she does in *Northanger Abbey*: "To begin perfect happiness at the respective ages of twenty-six and eighteen is to do pretty well." It's easy to see why we have come to believe that the fulfillment of life is love and marriage, and that in stepping through those portals, we will find the world magically changed from black-and-white to Technicolor, just as it was in *The Wizard of Oz*.

A novel, like a dream, is a never-never land where our fantasies can be indulged and miracles happen. Having entered this other world, we expect that things will end better than they do in our own, and so we will endure any amount of anguish and concern for the hero as long as there is the promise of a light at the end of the story. Every author is well aware of the reader's expectation that all should turn out happily for the hero, and, being in love with his or her own characters, the author probably wishes the same—until those characters persuade him otherwise. There the dilemma arises. Who is to be pleased: the reader or the author?

Experimenting with novel writing in the mid-1800s, Thomas Hardy followed the prescribed formula for happy endings until he had achieved stature enough to end his stories as *he* wished and his characters and the Fates demanded. But even Hardy was forced to alter the manuscript of *Tess of the D'Urbervilles* for magazine serialization, later restoring for the book version language and episodes deemed unfit for the eyes of lady magazine readers. The same ladies, reading the young Rudyard Kipling's novella *The Light That Failed* in the January 1891 *Lippincott's Monthly Magazine*, probably smiled tearfully over the requisite happy but somewhat insipid ending: the blinded artist hero, Dick Heldar, finally engaged to his childhood sweetheart, Maisie, who will selflessly care for him ever after. For this first attempt at novel writing, Kipling had apparently altered the ending on the advice of his American friend and future brother-in-law, the literary agent Wolcott Balestier. But Kipling returned to his original intention in the book version, which contained four additional chapters and a new, unhappy ending: Dick, blind and abandoned by Maisie, his one masterpiece destroyed by the vengeful model Bessie, in one last heroic effort follows his friends to the war in the Sudan, and invites his own death from a bullet to the head. There is no question about which is the better ending, and Kipling knew it.

The Victorians assured us that the hero would live "happily ever after" through a last paragraph or two that glimpsed a perfect future in some detail. This paragraph had the convenience of neatly tying up all the plot's ends and pieces and disposing of those matters that didn't interest the author enough to make them part of the story. Eventually this paragraph was replaced by an entire chapter, the epilogue, which leaped ahead in time to show us what had happened in the years since the end of the story. The epilogue satisfied our curiosity, particularly if the final chapter left the ending in question. Hopefully, its disposition of the characters was not so transparent that the reader would feel betrayed. I myself remember feeling so cheated by the ending to Tom Wolfe's *The Bonfire of the Vanities* that I closed the book (fortunately, a paperback), and threw it across the room. I am not a violent person; my protest was an instinctive reaction against Wolfe's leading me on and then choosing an easy way out, a glib resolution of characters that I felt was intrinsically false. For, even if the ending is not happy, it must at least seem true.

Of course, a happy ending doesn't always have to take the form of romantic love. Happiness can be the peace that follows conflict, the relief of tension after a rescue, the serenity that comes with self-acceptance, the contentment found in the warmth of the family. "Touched to the heart," reads the end of *Little Women*, "Mrs. March could only stretch out her arms as if to gather children and grandchildren to herself, and say, with face and voice full of motherly love, gratitude, and humility, 'O my girls, however long you may live, I never can wish you a greater happiness than this!'"

With this fervent wish warming our hearts, let us examine some great endings, beginning with the fairy tale "happily ever after."

'Til Death Us Do Part ✪
The lovers make an eternal vow.

"But don't you want to marry *me?*"

"There's no one else I would marry."

"Then that settles it."

"Mother and Dad will be surprised, won't they?"

"I'm so happy."

"I want my lunch," she said.

"Dear!"

He smiled and took her hand and pressed it. They got up and walked out of the gallery. They stood for a moment at the balustrade and looked at Trafalgar Square. Cabs and omnibuses hurried to and fro, and crowds passed, hastening in every direction, and the sun was shining.

—W. SOMERSET MAUGHAM, *Of Human Bondage*

"Faith," said Coggan, in a critical tone, turning to his companions, "the man hev learnt to say 'my wife' in a wonderful naterel way, considering how very youthful he is in wedlock as yet—hey, neighbours all?"

"I never heerd a skilful old married feller of twenty years' standing pipe 'my wife' in a more used note than 'a did," said Jacob Smallbury. "It might have been a little more true to nater if't had been spoke a little chillier, but that wasn't to be expected just now."

"That improvement will come wi' time," said Jan, twirling his eye.

Then Oak laughed, and Bathsheba smiled (for she never laughed readily now), and their friends turned to go.

"Yes; I suppose that's the size o't," said Joseph Poorgrass with a cheerful sigh as they moved away; "and I wish him joy o' her; though I were once or twice upon saying to-day with holy Hosea, in my scripture manner, which is my second nature, 'Ephraim is joined to idols: let him alone.' But since 'tis as 'tis, why, it might have been worse, and I feel my thanks accordingly."

—THOMAS HARDY, *Far from the Madding Crowd*

(George Emerson suggests to his new wife, Lucy Honeychurch, that despite all her efforts to keep them apart, her chaperone and cousin, Miss Bartlett, had really meant all along for them to be together.)
". . . Look how she kept me alive in you all the summer; how she gave you no peace; how month after month she became more eccentric and unreliable. The sight of us haunted her—or she couldn't have described us as she did to her friend. There are details—it burnt. I read the book afterwards. She is not frozen, Lucy, she is not withered up all through. She tore us apart twice, but in the Rectory that evening she was given one more chance to make us happy. We can never make friends with her or thank her. But I do believe that, far down in her heart, far below all speech and behaviour, she is glad."

"It is impossible," murmured Lucy, and then, remembering the experiences of her own heart, she said: "No—it is just possible."

Youth enwrapped them; the song of Phaethon announced passion requited, love attained. But they were conscious of a love more mysterious than this. The song died away; they heard the river, bearing down the snows of winter into the Mediterranean.

—E. M. FORSTER, *A Room With a View*

"My heart never kissed any other man but you!" she cried. "How often and often and often have I kissed you, and you never knew! . . . It was for a message that I sent George down here—a message to you! . . . I named him after you. . . .

Do you think that if dreams could make him your child—he wouldn't be yours—?"

Her courage, and the expression of it, seemed to him to be sublime.

"You don't know me!" she sighed, less convulsively.

"Don't I!" he said with lofty confidence.

After a whole decade his nostrils quivered again to the odour of her olive skin. Drowning amid the waves of her terrible devotion, he was recompensed in the hundredth part of a second for all that through her he had suffered or might hereafter suffer. The many problems and difficulties which marriage with her would raise seemed trivial in the light of her heart's magnificent and furious loyalty. He thought of the younger Edwin whom she had kissed into rapture, as of a boy too inexperienced in sorrow to appreciate this Hilda. He braced himself to the exquisite burden of life.

—ARNOLD BENNETT, *Clayhanger*

(Maggie eases a reconciliation with her Italian prince husband, Amerigo, by speaking kindly of his former lover, her own father's second wife, Charlotte.)

"Isn't she too spendid?" she simply said, offering it to explain and to finish.

"Oh, splendid!" With which he came over to her.

"That's our help, you see," she added—to point further her moral.

It kept him before her therefore, taking in—or trying to— what she so wonderfully gave. He tried, too clearly, to please her—to meet her in her own way; but with the result only that, close to her, her face kept before him, his hands holding her shoulders, his whole act enclosing her, he presently echoed: " 'See'? I see nothing but *you*." And the truth of it had, with this force, after a moment, so strangely lighted his eyes that, as for pity and dread of them, she buried her own in his breast.

—HENRY JAMES, *The Golden Bowl*

"Glad to part again, Estella? To me parting is a painful thing. To me, the remembrance of our last parting has been ever mournful and painful."

"But you said to me," returned Estella, very earnestly, " 'God bless you, God forgive you!' And if you could say that to me then, you will not hesitate to say that to me now—now, when suffering has been stronger than all other teaching, and has taught me to understand what your heart used to be. I have been bent and broken, but—I hope—into a better shape. Be as considerate and good to me as you were, and tell me we are friends."

"We are friends," said I, rising and bending over her, as she rose from the bench.

"And will continue friends apart," said Estella.

I took her hand in mine, and we went out of the ruined place; and, as the morning mists had risen long ago when I first left the forge, so, the evening mists were rising now, and in all the broad expanse of tranquil light they showed to me, I saw no shadow of another parting from her.

—CHARLES DICKENS, *Great Expectations*

Future Perfect ❦
A view into the crystal ball.

Lady Catherine was extremely indignant on the marriage of her nephew; and as she gave way to all the genuine frankness of her character, in her reply to the letter which announced its arrangement, she sent him language so very abusive, especially of Elizabeth, that for some time all intercourse was at an end. But at length, by Elizabeth's persuasion, he was prevailed on to overlook the offence, and seek a reconciliation; and, after a little further resistance on the part of his aunt, her resentment gave way, either to her affection for him, or her curiosity to see how his wife conducted herself: and she condescended to wait on them at Pemberley, in spite of that pollution which its woods had received, not merely from the presence of such a mistress, but the visits of her uncle and aunt from the city.

With the Gardiners they were always on the most intimate terms. Darcy, as well as Elizabeth, really loved them; and they were both ever sensible of the warmest gratitude towards the persons who, by bringing her into Derbyshire, had been the means of uniting them.

—JANE AUSTEN, *Pride and Prejudice*

Mrs. Dashwood was prudent enough to remain at the cottage, without attempting a removal to Delaford; and fortunately for Sir John and Mrs. Jennings, when Marianne was taken from them, Margaret had reached an age highly suitable for dancing, and not very ineligible for being supposed to have a lover.

Between Barton and Delaford, there was that constant communication which strong family affection would naturally dictate; and among the merits and the happiness of Elinor and Marianne, let it not be ranked as the least considerable, that though sisters, and living almost within sight of each other, they could live without disagreement between themselves, or producing coolness between their husbands.

—JANE AUSTEN, *Sense and Sensibility*

The result of this distress, was, that, with a much more voluntary, cheerful consent than his daughter had ever presumed to hope for at the moment, she was able to fix her wedding-day; and Mr. Elton was called on, within a month from the marriage of Mr. and Mrs. Robert Martin, to join the hands of Mr. Knightley and Miss Woodhouse.

The wedding was very much like other weddings, where the parties have no taste for finery or parade; and Mrs. Elton, from the particulars detailed by her husband, thought it all extremely shabby, and very inferior to her own. "Very little white satin, very few lace veils; a most pitiful business! Selina would stare when she heard of it." But, in spite of these deficiencies, the wishes, the hopes, the confidence, the predictions of the small band of true friends who witnessed the ceremony, were fully answered in the perfect happiness of the union.

—JANE AUSTEN, *Emma*

As you look at Wendy you may see her hair becoming white, and her figure little again, for all this happened long ago. Jane is now a common grown-up, with a daughter called Margaret; and every spring-cleaning time, except when he forgets, Peter comes for Margaret and takes her to the Neverland, where she tells him stories about himself, to which he listens eagerly. When Margaret grows up she will have a daughter, who is to be Peter's mother in turn; and so it will go on, so long as children are gay and innocent and heartless.

—J. M. BARRIE, *Peter and Wendy*

(Jane Eyre, after fleeing from Thornfield, is rescued by the Reverend St. John Rivers and his sisters, who are revealed to be her cousins. Before Jane can decline Rivers's proposal of marriage, a dream calls her back to a blinded Mr. Rochester; in her happiness with him, she reflects on the minister's fate.)

St. John is unmarried: he never will marry now. Himself has hitherto sufficed to the toil; and the toil draws near its close: his glorious sun hastens to its setting. The last letter I received from him drew from my eyes human tears, and yet filled my heart with Divine joy: he anticipated his sure reward, his incorruptible crown. I know that a stranger's hand will write to me next, to say that the good and faithful servant has been called at length into the joy of his Lord. And why weep for this? No fear of death will darken St. John's last hour: his mind will be unclouded; his heart will be undaunted; his hope will be sure; his faith steadfast. His own words are a pledge of this:—

The last page of the original manuscript of Charlotte Brontë's *Jane Eyre. (The British Library, Add. 43, 476-f.265)*

"My Master," he says, "has forewarned me. Daily he announces more distinctly,—'Surely I come quickly!' and hourly I more eagerly respond,—'Amen; even so come, Lord Jesus!'"

—CHARLOTTE BRONTË, *Jane Eyre*

. . . Mr. Pickwick is somewhat infirm now; but he retains all his former juvenility of spirit, and may still be frequently seen, contemplating the pictures in the Dulwich Gallery, or enjoying a walk about the pleasant neighbourhood on a fine day. He is known by all the poor people about, who never fail to take their hats off, as he passes, with great respect; the children idolize him; and so indeed does the whole neighbourhood. Every year, he repairs to a large family merry-making at Mr. Wardle's; on this, as on all other occasions, he is invariably attended by the faithful Sam, between whom and his master there exists a steady and reciprocal attachment, which nothing but death will terminate.

—CHARLES DICKENS, *The Posthumous Papers of the Pickwick Club*

Tom's most well now, and got his bullet around his neck on a watch-guard for a watch, and is always seeing what time it is, and so there ain't nothing more to write about, and I am rotten glad of it, because if I'd 'a' knowed what a trouble it was to make a book I wouldn't 'a' tackled it, and ain't a-going to no more. But I reckon I got to light out for the territory ahead of the rest, because Aunt Sally she's going to adopt me and sivilize me, and I can't stand it. I been there before.

—MARK TWAIN, *The Adventures of Huckleberry Finn*

Future Almost Perfect 🦎
Happiness of a sort.

(About two years after Quasimodo's mysterious disappearance and the execution of Esmeralda, in the cave of Montfaucon, where the bodies of the guilty and innocent were thrown . . .)

. . . there were found amongst all those hideous carcases two skeletons, the arms of one of which were thrown round the other. One of the two, that of a woman, had still about it some tattered fragments of a garment, apparently of a stuff that had once been white; and about its neck was a string of grains of adrezarach, together with a small silken bag, ornamented with green glass, which was open and empty. These articles had been of so little value that the executioner, doubtless, had not cared to take them. The other skeleton, which held this one close in its arms, was that of a man. It was remarked in the latter that the spine was crooked, the head compressed between the shoulder-blades, and that one leg was shorter than the other. It was also remarkable that there was no rupture of the vertebræ at the nape of the neck, whence it was evident that he had not been hanged. Hence it was inferred that the man must have come hither of himself and died here. When they strove to detach this skeleton from the one it was embracing, it fell to dust.

—VICTOR HUGO, *Notre-Dame de Paris*

Yeobright had, in fact, found his vocation in the career of an itinerant open-air preacher and lecturer on morally unimpeachable subjects; and from this day he laboured incessantly in that office, speaking not only in simple language on Rainbarrow and in the hamlets round, but in a more cultivated strain elsewhere—from the steps and porticoes of town-halls, from market-crosses, from conduits, on esplanades and on wharves, from the parapets of bridges, in barns and outhouses, and all other such places in the neighbouring Wessex towns and villages. He left alone creeds and systems of philosophy, finding enough and more than enough to occupy his tongue in the opinions and actions common to all good men. Some believed him, and some believed not; some said that his words were commonplace, others complained of his want of theological doctrine; while others again remarked that it was well enough for a man to take to preaching who could not see to do anything else. But everywhere he was kindly received, for the story of his life had become generally known.

—THOMAS HARDY, *The Return of the Native*

The same fate attended Judith. When Hawkeye reached the garrison on the Mohawk, he inquired anxiously after that lovely, but misguided creature. None knew her—even her person was no longer remembered. Other officers had again and again succeeded the Warleys and Craigs and Grahams; though an old sergeant of the garrison, who had lately come from England, was enabled to tell our hero that Sir Robert Warley lived on his paternal estates, and that there was a lady of rare beauty in the lodge, who had great influence over him, though she did not bear his name. Whether this was Judith, relapsed into her early failing, or some other victim of the soldier's, Hawkeye never knew, nor would it be pleasant or profitable to inquire. We live in a world of transgressions and selfishness, and no pictures that represent us otherwise can be true; though happily for human nature, gleamings of that pure spirit in whose likeness man has been fashioned, are to be seen, relieving its deformities, and mitigating, if not excusing its crimes.

—JAMES FENIMORE COOPER, *The Deerslayer*

To the Rescue ❦
The danger is over, and the hero safe and sound.

None the less, he knew that the tale he had to tell could not be one of a final victory. It could be only the record of what had had to be done, and what assuredly would have to be done again in the never ending fight against terror and its relentless onslaughts, despite their personal afflictions, by all who, while unable to be saints but

refusing to bow down to pestilences, strive their utmost
to be healers.

And, indeed, as he listened to the cries of joy rising from
the town, Rieux remembered that such joy is always imper-
iled. He knew what those jubilant crowds did not know but
could have learned from books: that the plague bacillus never
dies or disappears for good; that it can lie dormant for years
and years in furniture and linen-chests; that it bides its time
in bedrooms, cellars, trunks, and bookshelves; and that perhaps the day would come when, for the bane and the
enlightening of men, it would rouse up its rats again and
send them forth to die in a happy city.

—ALBERT CAMUS, *The Plague,* trans. Stuart Gilbert

*(The schoolboys, with their leader, Ralph, are found on the desert
island on which they had struggled to survive after an airplane crash.)*
Ralph looked at him dumbly. For a moment he had a fleeting picture of the strange glamour that had once invested the
beaches. But the island was scorched up like dead wood—
Simon was dead—and Jack had. . . . The tears began to flow
and sobs shook him. He gave himself up to them now for
the first time on the island; great, shuddering spasms of grief
that seemed to wrench his whole body. His voice rose under
the black smoke before the burning wreckage of the island;
and infected by that emotion, the other little boys began to
shake and sob too. And in the middle of them, with filthy
body, matted hair, and unwiped nose, Ralph wept for the
end of innocence, the darkness of man's heart, and the fall
through the air of the true, wise friend called Piggy.

The officer, surrounded by these noises, was moved and a little embarrassed. He turned away to give them time to pull themselves together; and waited, allowing his eyes to rest on the trim cruiser in the distance.

—WILLIAM GOLDING, *Lord of the Flies*

Aunt Em had just come out of the house to water the cabbages when she looked up and saw Dorothy running toward her.

"My darling child!" she cried, folding the little girl in her arms and covering her face with kisses, "where in the world did you come from?"

"From the Land of Oz," said Dorothy gravely. "And here is Toto, too. And oh, Aunt Em! I'm so glad to be at home again!"

—L. FRANK BAUM, *The Wizard of Oz*

(With no money for food, Ma Joad asks her daughter, who has just delivered a stillborn child, to save a sick and starving young man they find in a sheltering barn.)

For a minute Rose of Sharon sat still in the whispering barn. Then she hoisted her tired body up and drew the comforter about her. She moved slowly to the corner and stood looking down at the wasted face, into the wide, frightened eyes. Then slowly she lay down beside him. He shook his head slowly from side to side. Rose of Sharon loosened one side of the blanket and bared her breast. "You got to," she said. She squirmed closer and pulled his head close. "There!" she said. "There." Her hand moved behind his head and supported it. Her fingers moved gently in his hair. She looked up and across

the barn, and her lips came together and smiled mysteriously.
—JOHN STEINBECK, *The Grapes of Wrath*

(The ship arrives in Germany from Mexico in 1931 with its motley collection of passengers after a twenty-seven-day voyage and a man overboard.) The band played "Tannenbaum" at last, and kept it up until the gangplank was down, and the passengers began to descend rapidly and silently. As the musicians were wiping the mouthpieces of their instruments, wrapping up their drums and putting away their fiddles, their mouths were wide with smiles, their heads towards the dock, towards the exact narrow spot where the *Vera* had warped in and cast her anchor. Among them, a gangling young boy, who looked as if he had never had enough to eat in his life, nor a kind word from anybody, and did not know what he was going to do next, stared with blinded eyes, his mouth quivering while he shook the spit out of his trumpet, repeating to himself just above a whisper, *"Grüss Gott, Grüss Gott,"* as if the town were a human being, a good and dear trusted friend who had come a long way to welcome him.
—KATHERINE ANNE PORTER, *Ship of Fools*

Triumph 🎔
Great and small successes of the spirit.

Quickly, as if she were recalled by something over there, she turned to her canvas. There it was—her picture. Yes, with all its greens and blues, its lines running up and across, its attempt at something. It would be hung in the attics, she thought; it would be destroyed. But what did that matter? she asked herself, taking up her brush again. She looked at the steps; they were empty; she looked at her canvas; it was blurred. With a sudden intensity, as if she saw it clear for a second, she drew a line there, in the centre. It was done; it was finished. Yes, she thought, laying down her brush in extreme fatigue, I have had my vision.

—VIRGINIA WOOLF, *To the Lighthouse*

(After the death of Dr. Juvenal Urbino fifty years after their marriage, his widow, Fermina Daza, is reunited with Florentino Ariza, whose love she had spurned for Urbino's position and wealth. On a riverboat trip, they finally consummate their love.)

The Captain looked at Fermina Daza and saw on her eyelashes the first glimmer of wintry frost. Then he looked at Florentino Ariza, his invincible power, his intrepid love, and he was overwhelmed by the belated suspicion that it is life, more than death, that has no limits.

"And how long do you think we can keep up this goddamn coming and going?" he asked.

Florentino Ariza had kept his answer ready for fifty-three years, seven months, and eleven days and nights.

"Forever," he said.

—GABRIEL GARCÍA MÁRQUEZ, *Love in the Time of Cholera,*
trans. Edith Grossman

(Lashed to the old fisherman's boat are the remains of the great marlin he has caught, which was ravaged by sharks as he returned from the sea.)
That afternoon there was a party of tourists at the Terrace and looking down in the water among the empty beer cans and dead barracudas a woman saw a great long white spine with a huge tail at the end that lifted and swung with the tide while the east wind blew a heavy steady sea outside the entrance to the harbour.

"What's that?" she asked a waiter and pointed to the long backbone of the great fish that was now just garbage waiting to go out with the tide.

"Tiburon," the waiter said, "Eshark." He was meaning to explain what had happened.

"I didn't know sharks had such handsome, beautifully formed tails."

"I didn't either," her male companion said.

Up the road, in his shack, the old man was sleeping again. He was still sleeping on his face and the boy was sitting by him watching him. The old man was dreaming about the lions.

—ERNEST HEMINGWAY, *The Old Man and the Sea*

But he is not always alone. When the long winter nights come on and the wolves follow their meat into the lower valleys, he may be seen running at the head of the pack through the pale moonlight or glimmering borealis, leaping gigantic above his fellows, his great throat a-bellow as he sings a song of the younger world, which is the song of the pack.

—JACK LONDON, *The Call of the Wild*

(The blinded Dick Heldar seeks death in the desert.)
"Get down, man! Get down behind the camel!"

"No. Put me, I pray, in the forefront of the battle." Dick turned his face to Torpenhow and raised his hand to set his helmet straight, but, miscalculating the distance, knocked it off. Torpenhow saw that his hair was grey on the temples, and that his face was the face of an old man.

"Come down, you damned fool! Dickie, come off!"

And Dick came obediently, but as a tree falls, pitching sideways from the Bisharin's saddle at Torpenhow's feet. His luck had held to the last, even to the crowning mercy of a kindly bullet through his head.

Torpenhow knelt under the lee of the camel, with Dick's body in his arms.

—RUDYARD KIPLING, *The Light That Failed*

Home Sweet Home 🦗
The cat's on the hearth and all is peace at last.

(The novel ends as it began, with a Letter to God.)
I feel a little peculiar round the children. For one thing, they grown. And I see they think me and Nettie and Shug and Albert and Samuel and Harpo and Sofia and Jack and Odessa real old and don't know much what going on. But I don't think us feel old at all. And us so happy. Matter of fact, I think this the youngest us ever felt.

Amen

—ALICE WALKER, *The Color Purple*

Detail from the original manuscript of the "happy ending" version of Rudyard Kipling's *The Light That Failed*, written for the January 1891 *Lippincott's Monthly Magazine* and later changed to the unhappy ending Kipling preferred in the book version. *(Frank N. Doubleday and Nelson Doubleday Collection, Manuscripts Division, Department of Rare Books and Special Collections, Princeton University Libraries)*

(Margaret asks her husband if it is true that his dead first wife had left the cottage, Howards End, to her.)

Tranquilly he replied: "Yes, she did. But that is a very old story. When she was ill and you were so kind to her, she wanted to make you some return, and, not being herself at the time, scribbled 'Howards End' on a piece of paper. I went into it thoroughly, and, as it was clearly fanciful, I set it aside, little knowing what my Margaret would be to me in the future."

Margaret was silent. Something shook her life in its inmost recesses, and she shivered.

"I didn't do wrong, did I?" he asked, bending down.

"You didn't, darling. Nothing has been done wrong."

From the garden came laughter. "Here they are at last!" exclaimed Henry, disengaging himself with a smile. Helen rushed into the gloom, holding Tom by one hand and carrying her baby on the other. There were shouts of infectious joy.

"The field's cut!" Helen cried excitedly—"the big meadow! We've seen to the very end, and it'll be such a crop of hay as never!"

—E. M. FORSTER, *Howards End*

"Yes, Jo, I think your harvest will be a good one," began Mrs. March, frightening away a big black cricket that was staring Teddy out of countenance.

"Not half so good as yours, mother. Here it is, and we

Detail of the last page of the original manuscript of E. M. Forster's *Howards End. (King's College Library, Cambridge)* never can thank you enough for the patient sowing and reaping you have done," cried Jo, with the loving impetuosity which she never could outgrow.

"I hope there will be more wheat and fewer tares every year," said Amy softly.

"A large sheaf, but I know there's room in your heart for it, Marmee dear," added Meg's tender voice.

Touched to the heart, Mrs. March could only stretch out her arms as if to gather children and grandchildren to herself, and say, with face and voice full of motherly love, gratitude, and humility, "O my girls, however long you may live, I never can wish you a greater happiness than this!"

—LOUISA MAY ALCOTT, *Little Women*

(Extract from a letter from George Lawrence Esq., C.M.G., of His Majesty's Nigerian Civil Service, to Colonel Henri de Beaujolais, XIXth African Army Corps. Michael "Beau" Geste has died, having confessed stealing a fake "Blue Water" stone that Lady Brandon, in fear of her late husband, had had made when she was forced to sell the real stone.)

"And the remaining piece of news is that I do most sincerely hope that you will be able to come over to England in June.

"You are the best man I know, Jolly, and I want you to be my Best Man, a desire heartily shared by Lady Brandon.

"Fancy, old cabbage, after more than thirty years of devotion! . . . I feel like a boy!

"And that fine boy, John, is going to marry the 'so beautiful child' whom you remembered. Lady Brandon is being a fairy godmother to them, indeed. I think she feels she is somehow doing something for Michael by smoothing their path so. . . ."
—PERCIVAL CHRISTOPHER WREN, *Beau Geste*

19 ❧ HOPE SPRINGS

argaret Mitchell is said to have written the last scene of *Gone With the Wind* first. It was a technique she had used in writing mystery stories, in which she worked backward from the solution to the crime, and although she was to rethink and eliminate many chapters of the book, this last scene remained intact. When her editor read the ending, in which Rhett has seemingly left his wife, Scarlett, forever, he felt it was too harsh. She agreed to soften it, but she refused to make it conventionally happy. After all, there was no doubt in Margaret Mitchell's mind that Scarlett would get Rhett back again. Her world may have come crashing down around her, but Scarlett had not given up, and the last words from her lips represent a final instance of her great courage, or as Margaret Mitchell herself called it, her "gumption." For Scarlett, whose strength came first from within, and then from the land, there was always tomorrow, always Tara, and therefore, always hope.

Hope makes a good breakfast, Henry Fielding notes in *Tom Jones*. Hope also makes a good ending, whether it comes to the hero innocently wronged or to the hero redeemed from a life of wickedness. Either way, it means that a lesson has been learned, and the hero has moved from the point at which we first met him to the point where we must leave him. This movement is a vital element of the novel, as it is of the drama, story ballet, and opera.

Hope is the hero turning his back on the life he has always lived and venturing into the world, like Joel Knox in Truman Capote's *Other Voices, Other Rooms*: "She beckoned to him, shining and silver, and he knew he must go: unafraid, not hesitating, he paused only at the garden's edge where, as though he'd forgotten something, he stopped and looked back at the bloomless, descending blue, at the boy he had left behind." Or marching into the sunset as in *The Peaceable Kingdom*, by Jan de Hartog: "The red speck of the feathers on his Quaker hat was the last of him to vanish in the infinite prairie of light and love." Hope is a timid heroine daring to try something of which she was not before capable, as in Booth Tarkington's *Alice Adams*: "She looked up and down the street quickly, and then, with a little heave of the shoulders, she went bravely in, under the sign, and began to climb the wooden steps. Half-way up the shadows were heaviest, but after that the place began to seem brighter. There was an open window overhead somewhere, she found, and the steps at the top were gay with sunshine."

Hope can mean redemption, as for Konstantine Levin in *Anna Karenina*: ". . . my life now, my whole life apart from anything that can happen to me, every minute of it is no more meaningless, as it was before, but it has the positive meaning of goodness, which I have the power to put into it." Or an awareness of the vastness of the universe or the insistent cycle of Nature as an omen of good, as with Mr. Lockwood in *Wuthering Heights*: "I lingered round them, under that benign sky: watched the moths fluttering among the heath and hare-bells; listened to the soft wind breathing through the grass; and wondered how any one could ever imagine unquiet slumbers for the sleepers in that quiet earth."

Finally, hope can be symbolic, as in Conrad's *An Outcast of the Islands*, where a drunken Almayer assaults the Night and the fugitive Willems:

> ". . . Where are you, Willems? Hey? . . . Hey? . . . Where there is no mercy for you—I hope!"
>
> "Hope," repeated in a whispering echo the startled forests, the river, and the hills; and Almayer, who stood waiting, with a smile of tipsy attention on his lips, heard no other answer.

Tomorrow and Tomorrow and Tomorrow ❦
The hero looks to a bright new day.

She felt vaguely comforted, strengthened by the picture, and some of her hurt and frantic regret was pushed from the top of her mind. She stood for a moment remembering small things, the avenue of dark cedars leading to Tara, the banks of cape jessamine bushes, vivid green against the white walls, the fluttering white curtains. And Mammy would be there. Suddenly she wanted Mammy desperately, as she had wanted her when she was a little girl, wanted the broad bosom on which to lay her head, the gnarled black hand on her hair. Mammy, the last link with the old days.

With the spirit of her people who would not know defeat, even when it stared them in the face, she raised her chin. She could get Rhett back. She knew she could. There had never been a man she couldn't get, once she set her mind upon him.

"I'll think of it all tomorrow, at Tara. I can stand it then. Tomorrow, I'll think of some way to get him back. After all, tomorrow is another day."

—MARGARET MITCHELL, *Gone With the Wind*

When I awoke it was early morning. I lay looking straight up at the blue-green sky with its translucent shawl of mist; like a tiny orb of crystal, solitary and serene, Venus shone through the haze above the quiet ocean. I heard children chattering nearby. I stirred. *"Izzy, he's awake!" "G'wan, yah mutha's mustache!" "Fuuu-ck you!"* Blessing my resurrection, I realized that the children had covered me with sand, protectively, and that I lay as safe as a mummy beneath this fine, enveloping overcoat. It was then that in my mind I inscribed the words: *'Neath cold sand I dreamed of death / but woke at dawn to see / in glory, the bright, the morning star.*

This was not judgment day—only morning. Morning: excellent and fair.

—WILLIAM STYRON, *Sophie's Choice*

. . . Naturally, at first it would only be a tedious, tiring job, it wouldn't prevent me from existing or from feeling that I exist. But a time would have to come when the book would be written, would be behind me, and I think that a little of its light would fall over my past. Then, through it, I might be able to recall my life without repugnance. Perhaps one day, thinking about this very moment, about this dismal moment at which I am waiting, round-shouldered, for it to be time to get on the train, perhaps I might feel my heart beat faster and say to myself: "It was on that day, at that moment that it all started." And I might succeed—in the past, simply in the past—in accepting myself.

Night is falling. On the first floor of the Hôtel Printania two windows have just lighted up. The yard of the New Station smells strongly of damp wood: tomorrow it will rain over Bouville.

—JEAN-PAUL SARTRE, *Nausea*

It was certain that, in days soon to come, I should go home, those feelings flooding back, as alive as ever in the past, as I thought of cables or telephone calls. As alive as ever in the past. That was the price of the "I" which would not die.

But I had lived with that so long. I had lived with much

else too, and now I could recognise it. This wasn't an end: though, if I had thought so, looking at the house, I should have needed to propitiate Fate, remembering so many others' luck, Francis Getliffe's and the rest, and the comparison with mine. I had lived with much else that I would have had, and begged to have, again. That night would be a happy one. This wasn't an end.

(Who would dare to look in the mirror of his future?)

There would be other nights when I should go to sleep, looking forward to tomorrow.

—C. P. SNOW, *Strangers and Brothers* [*Last Things*]

Hope Against Hope 🐝
The hero finds redemption.

(The gamekeeper writes a letter to his lover, Lady Constance Chatterley, while they are separated, waiting for the divorce that will unite them.)
"Never mind, never mind, we won't get worked up. We really trust in the little flame, in the unnamed god that shields it from being blown out. There's so much of you here with me, really, that it's a pity you aren't all here.

"Never mind about Sir Clifford. If you don't hear anything from him, never mind. He can't really do anything to you. Wait, he will want to get rid of you at last, to cast you out. And if he doesn't, we'll manage to keep clear of him. But he will. In the end he will want to spew you out as the abominable thing.

"Now I can't even leave off writing to you.

"But a great deal of us is together, and we can but abide by it, and steer our courses to meet soon. John Thomas says good night to lady Jane, a little droopingly, but with a hopeful heart."

—D. H. LAWRENCE, *Lady Chatterley's Lover*

(The wily English barrister Sydney Carton is redeemed by taking the place of the Frenchman Charles Darnay on the scaffold because of his devotion to Darnay's wife, Lucie.)

". . . I see her, an old woman, weeping for me on the anniversary of this day. I see her and her husband, their course done, lying side by side in their last earthly bed, and I know that each was not more honoured and held sacred in the other's soul, than I was in the souls of both.

"I see that child who lay upon her bosom and who bore my name, a man winning his way up in that path of life which once was mine. I see him winning it so well, that my name is made illustrious there by the light of his. I see the blots I threw upon it, faded away. I see him, foremost of just judges and honoured men, bringing a boy of my name, with a forehead that I know and golden hair, to this place—then fair to look upon, with not a trace of this day's disfigure-ment—and I hear him tell the child my story, with a tender and a faltering voice.

"It is a far, far better thing that I do, than I have ever done; it is a far, far better rest that I go to, than I have ever known."

—CHARLES DICKENS, *A Tale of Two Cities*

In time he lay down on his bed looking at the ceiling curiously, a splotch of brown—a leak in the roof, no doubt. As he began to observe the marks on the ceiling, gradually the inner agitation, the troubled surface of his mind, grew quiet. One by one the voices were silenced. He thought of that last conversation. The thing he could do for her, the whole meaning of their relationship, he saw would lie in his work. And there is so much to do, he thought. There is so much to do that I must begin at once. Where there is action possible there can be no despair.

The loneliness would come later. It is harder to get beyond it. But in the end he would come to see that one does not find this kind of love, built on understanding, and ever lose it. It would not matter now where he was, she would always be there. It was a way of living he had found. It was the means of living, not with her, but with himself.

—MAY SARTON, *The Single Hound*

So it came to pass that as he trudged from the place of blood and wrath his soul changed. He came from hot plowshares to prospects of clover tranquilly, and it was as if hot plowshares were not. Scars faded as flowers.

It rained. The procession of weary soldiers became a bedraggled train, despondent and muttering, marching with churning effort in a trough of liquid brown mud under a low, wretched sky. Yet the youth smiled, for he saw that the world was a world for him, though many discovered it to be made of oaths and walking sticks. He had rid himself of the red sickness of battle. The sultry nightmare was in the past. He had been an animal blistered and sweating in the heat and pain of war. He turned now with a lover's thirst to images of tranquil skies, fresh meadows, cool brooks—an existence of soft and eternal peace.

Over the river a golden ray of sun came through the hosts of leaden rain clouds.

—STEPHEN CRANE, *The Red Badge of Courage*

"This new feeling has not changed me, has not made me happy and enlightened all of a sudden, as I had dreamed, just like the feeling for my child. There was no surprise in this either. Faith—or not faith—I don't know what it is—but this feeling has come just as imperceptibly through suffering, and has taken firm root in my soul.

"I shall go on in the same way, losing my temper with Ivan the coachman, falling into angry discussions, expressing my opinions tactlessly; there will be still the same wall between the holy of holies of my soul and other people, even my wife; I shall still go on scolding her for my own terror, and being remorseful for it; I shall still be as unable to under-stand with my reason why I pray, and I shall still go on pray-ing; but my life now, my whole life apart from anything that can happen to me, every minute of it is no more meaning-less, as it was before, but it has the positive meaning of good-ness, which I have the power to put into it."

—COUNT LEO TOLSTOY, *Anna Karenina,*
trans. Constance Garnett

Into the Sunset ❦
In search of happiness, the hero leaves for parts unknown.

And day came, and the song of waking birds, and the Square, bathed in the young pearl light of morning. And a wind stirred lightly in the Square, and, as he looked, Ben, like a fume of smoke, was melted into dawn.

And the angels on Gant's porch were frozen in hard marble silence, and at a distance life awoke, and there was a rattle of lean wheels, a slow clangor of shod hoofs. And he heard the whistle wail along the river.

Yet, as he stood for the last time by the angels of his father's porch, it seemed as if the Square already were far and lost; or, I should say, he was like a man who stands upon a hill above the town he has left, yet does not say "The town is near," but turns his eyes upon the distant soaring ranges.

—THOMAS WOLFE, *Look Homeward, Angel*

His mind was absolutely clear. He was like a camera waiting for its subject to enter focus. The wall yellowed in the meticulous setting of the October sun, and the windows were rippling mirrors of cold, seasonal color. Beyond one, someone was watching him. All of him was dumb except his eyes. They knew. And it was Randolph's window. Gradually the blinding sunset drained from the glass, darkened, and it was as if snow were falling there, flakes shaping snow-eyes, hair: a face trembled like a white beautiful moth, smiled. She beckoned to him, shining and silver, and he knew he must go:

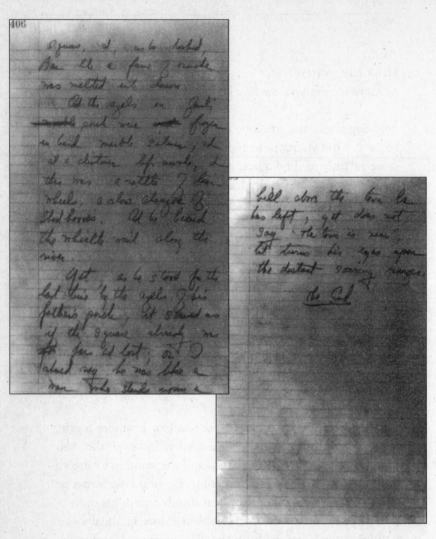

The last two pages of the original notebook manuscript of Thomas Wolfe's *Look Homeward, Angel. (Houghton Library, Harvard University, bMS Am 1883 [194–210])*

unafraid, not hesitating, he paused only at the garden's edge where, as though he'd forgotten something, he stopped and looked back at the bloomless, descending blue, at the boy he had left behind.

—TRUMAN CAPOTE, *Other Voices, Other Rooms*

So I had my last lunch at home, with my mother and Uncle Bhakcu and his wife. Then back along the hot road to Piarco where the plane was waiting. I recognized one of the customs' officers, and he didn't check my baggage.

The announcement came, a cold, casual thing.

I embraced my mother.

I said to Bhakcu, "Uncle Bhak, I didn't want to tell you before, but I think I hear your tappet knocking."

His eyes shone.

I left them all and walked briskly towards the aeroplane, not looking back, looking only at my shadow before me, a dancing dwarf on the tarmac.

—V. S. NAIPAUL, *Miguel Street*

And at last I step out into the morning and I lock the door behind me. I cross the road and drop the keys into the old lady's mailbox. And I look up the road, where a few people stand, men and women, waiting for the morning bus. They are very vivid beneath the awakening sky, and the horizon beyond them is beginning to flame. The morning weighs on my shoulders with the dreadful weight of hope and I take the blue envelope which Jacques has sent me and tear it slowly into many pieces, watching them dance in the wind, watching the wind carry them away. Yet, as I turn and begin walking toward the waiting people, the wind blows some of them back on me.

—JAMES BALDWIN, *Giovanni's Room*

By midnight he had left the road and the burning woods behind him and had come out on the highway once more. The moon, riding low above the field beside him, appeared and disappeared, diamond-bright, between patches of darkness. Intermittently the boy's jagged shadow slanted across the road ahead of him as if it cleared a rough path toward his goal. His singed eyes, black in their deep sockets, seemed already to envision the fate that awaited him but he moved steadily on, his face set toward the dark city, where the children of God lay sleeping.

—FLANNERY O'CONNOR, *The Violent Bear It Away*

He sat for a long time on the bench in the thickening dusk, his eyes never turning from the balcony. At length a light shone through the windows, and a moment later a man-servant came out on the balcony, drew up the awnings, and closed the shutters.

At that, as if it had been the signal he waited for, Newland Archer got up slowly and walked back alone to his hotel.

—EDITH WHARTON, *The Age of Innocence*

The last two pages of an early outline of Edith Wharton's *The Age of Innocence*, in which Newland Archer marries, then separates from, Countess Olenska, and "May Welland marries some one else & nothing ever happens to him again." *(Yale Collection of American Literature, Beinecke Rare Book and Manuscript Library, Yale University)*

Heaven Knows 🦎
Solace comes from the benign universe.

My walk home was lengthened by a diversion in the direction of the kirk. When beneath its walls, I perceived decay
had made progress, even in seven months: many a window
showed black gaps deprived of glass; and slates jutted off,
here and there, beyond the right line of the roof, to be gradually worked off in coming autumn storms.

I sought, and soon discovered, the three headstones on the
slope next the moor: the middle one grey, and half buried in
heath; Edgar Linton's only harmonized by the turf, and moss
creeping up its foot; Heathcliff's still bare.

I lingered round them, under that benign sky: watched the
moths fluttering among the heath and hare-bells; listened to
the soft wind breathing through the grass; and wondered
how any one could ever imagine unquiet slumbers for the
sleepers in that quiet earth.

—EMILY BRONTË, *Wuthering Heights*

With death so near, Mother must have felt like someone on
the brink of freedom, ready to start life all over again. No one,
no one in the world had any right to weep for her. And I, too,
felt ready to start life all over again. It was as if that great rush
of anger had washed me clean, emptied me of hope, and, gaz-
ing up at the dark sky spangled with its signs and stars, for the
first time, the first, I laid my heart open to the benign indifference of the universe. To feel it so like myself, indeed, so

brotherly, made me realize that I'd been happy, and that I was happy still. For all to be accomplished, for me to feel less lonely, all that remained to hope was that on the day of my execution there should be a huge crowd of spectators and that they should greet me with howls of execration.

—ALBERT CAMUS, *The Stranger,* trans. Stuart Gilbert

. . . So quietly flows the Seine that one hardly notices its presence. It is always there, quiet and unobtrusive, like a great artery running through the human body. In the wonderful peace that fell over me it seemed as if I had climbed to the top of a high mountain; for a little while I would be able to look around me, to take in the meaning of the landscape.

Human beings make a strange fauna and flora. From a distance they appear negligible; close up they are apt to appear ugly and malicious. More than anything they need to be surrounded with sufficient space—space even more than time.

The sun is setting. I feel this river flowing through me—its past, its ancient soil, the changing climate. The hills gently girdle it about: its course is fixed.

—HENRY MILLER, *Tropic of Cancer*

Yes, it is the dawn that has come. The titihoya wakes from sleep, and goes about its work of forlorn crying. The sun tips with light the mountains of Ingeli and East Griqualand. The great valley of the Umzimkulu is still in darkness, but the light will come there. Ndotsheni is still in darkness, but the light will come there also. For it is the dawn that has come, as it has come for a thousand centuries, never failing. But when that dawn will come, of our emancipation, from the fear of bondage and the bondage of fear, why, that is a secret.

—ALAN PATON, *Cry, the Beloved Country*

... If, at least, there were granted me time enough to complete my work, I would not fail to stamp it with the seal of that Time the understanding of which was this day so forcibly impressing itself upon me, and I would therein describe men—even should that give them the semblance of monstrous creatures—as occupying in Time a place far more considerable than the so restricted one allotted them in space, a place, on the contrary, extending boundlessly since, giant-like, reaching far back into the years, they touch simultaneously epochs of their lives—with countless intervening days between—so widely separated from one another in Time.

—MARCEL PROUST, *Remembrance of Things Past*
[*The Past Recaptured*],
trans. Frederick A. Blossom

20 ❧ UNHAPPILY EVER AFTER

magine the opera *Otello* ending with a love duet instead of a murder, the Moor having accepted Desdemona's avowal of innocence. Or a *Rigoletto* in which the jester's daughter Gilda, stabbed and dying in her father's arms, miraculously recovers. Or a *Carmen* in which the gypsy girl is allowed to survive to a tempestuous old age.

In the nineteenth century, Italian opera was performed with just such conclusions, last scenes that seem inconceivable to us now. In fact, composers were under great pressure to write the *lieto fine*, or happy ending, in which good was rewarded, fate and circumstance laughed at, and only the villain destroyed. Audiences of the time demanded these artistic compromises; in England, too, Shakespearean tragedies were rewritten to end happily. Yet it is interesting that *Otello*, *Rigoletto*, and *Carmen*—and the Shakespeare plays—have survived as we know them, with the sacrifice of innocence and goodness to passion and vengeance, and all the cathartic qualities of true tragedy.

One reason for this is undoubtedly that tragedy is simply more dramatic. Any television news show is proof of that. But another is that in its own way, the unhappy ending can be as satisfying as the happy ending. It is an acceptable denouement to an unlikely relationship or a situation that even the author cannot imagine continuing. Especially during and following the Victorian period, it was a way to justify the portrayal of an "immoral" hero: Hardy's Tess, driven to murdering the man who has ruined her, must hang; Flaubert's Emma Bovary, desperately grasping at happiness in adulterous affairs, must take poison; Conrad's Lord Jim, having once abandoned the passengers on a doomed pilgrim ship, must atone for his cowardice in seeking an honorable death.

Endings like these that conclude with the hero's death allow the author, having entangled the hero irreparably, to resolve those entanglements cleanly and dramatically. In fact, death comes almost as a relief to the life the hero has been leading, even as a moral victory and a triumph. If the hero is spared the ultimate punishment of death, he must at least atone for his fall from grace and vow to live a purer existence. Few heroes are permitted to get away, literally or figuratively, with murder.

Of course, the hero must be a hero in the classical sense: not too perfect but not too evil, noble but with a tragic flaw. We can accept a tragic ending because of the catharsis we experience, that is: we have identified with the hero, suffered with him, pitied him, felt awe as he stood against Fate or catastrophe, exulted as he changed or grew, and triumphed with him as he upheld his ideals even unto death. *La commedia è finita*, our emotions have been totally spent; our souls cleansed, and contrary to what we would expect at such an unhappy outcome, we are not angry or depressed, but elated.

Although death is the consummate unhappy ending, it is not the only one. The separation of lovers, the destruction of a self-consuming ambition, the prospect of a lonely old age—all leave the characters and vicariously, the reader, sadder but wiser. We shall look at death in another chapter, but first, here are selections from novels that end in less finite "unhappily ever afters."

La Commedia È Finita 🦋
The hero's trials are mercifully at an end.

Upon the cornice of the tower a tall staff was fixed. Their eyes were riveted on it. A few minutes after the hour had struck something moved slowly up the staff, and extended itself upon the breeze. It was a black flag.

"Justice" was done, and the President of the Immortals (in Æschylean phrase) had ended his sport with Tess. And the D'Urberville knights and dames slept on in their tombs unknowing. The two speechless gazers bent themselves down to the earth, as if in prayer, and remained thus a long time, absolutely motionless: the flag continued to wave silently. As soon as they had strength they arose, joined hands again, and went on.

—THOMAS HARDY, *Tess of the D'Urbervilles*

(Kit Sorrell, who has become a doctor through his father's lifelong labor and sacrifice, hastens the death of the terminally ill man.)
Kit went to the window, and while he was standing there a long pause came in the flow of his father's breathing. Kit's own breathing seemed to pause with it. Again, it was resumed, but very gently, and with a rustling and pathetic serenity. Life was passing, and all the pain and the stress were passing with it.

The window grew more grey. Kit could distinguish the branches and the foliage of the old pear tree black against the gradual dawn. And suddenly, he turned quickly and looked towards the bed. His father's breathing had ceased; he saw the dim face on the pillow. The stillness held.

Kit turned again to the window where the grey world was coming to life before eyes that were wet and blurred.

—WARWICK DEEPING, *Sorrell and Son*

(Frederic Henry, an American who had fallen in love with an English nurse while an ambulance driver in Italy during World War I, loses her and their son in childbirth in a Swiss hospital. The doctor tries to help.)
"Good-night," he said. "I cannot take you to your hotel?"

"No, thank you."

"It was the only thing to do," he said. "The operation proved—"

"I do not want to talk about it," I said.

"I would like to take you to your hotel."

"No, thank you."

He went down the hall. I went to the door of the room.

"You can't come in now," one of the nurses said.

"Yes I can," I said.

"You can't come in yet."

"You get out," I said. "The other one too."

But after I had got them out and shut the door and turned off the light it wasn't any good. It was like saying good-by to a statue. After a while I went out and left the hospital and walked back to the hotel in the rain.

—ERNEST HEMINGWAY, *A Farewell to Arms*

(The peak of the volcano, Popocatepetl, rises above the bar from which Mexican villagers throw the alcoholic British ex-consul, Geoffrey Firmin, to his death.)

. . . Strong hands lifted him. Opening his eyes, he looked down, expecting to see, below him, the magnificent jungle, the heights, Pico de Orizabe, Malinche, Cofre de Perote, like those peaks of his life conquered one after another before this greatest ascent of all had been successfully, if unconventionally, completed. But there was nothing there: no peaks, no life, no climb. Nor was this summit a summit exactly: it had no substance, no firm base. It was crumbling too, whatever it was, collapsing, while he was falling, falling into the volcano, he must have climbed it after all, though now there was this noise of foisting lava in his ears, horribly, it was in eruption, yet no, it wasn't the volcano, the world itself was bursting, bursting into black spouts of villages catapulted into space, with himself falling through it all, through the inconceivable pandemonium of a million tanks, through the blazing of ten million burning bodies, falling, into a forest, falling—

Suddenly he screamed, and it was as though this scream were being tossed from one tree to another, as its echoes returned, then, as though the trees themselves were crowding nearer, huddled together, closing over him, pitying . . .

Somebody threw a dead dog after him down the ravine.

—MALCOLM LOWRY, *Under the Volcano*

(Mrs. Moresby, rescued from her ordeal in the Moroccan desert, is delivered to a hotel in Marrakesh. Crazed, she is momentarily left alone in the cab.)

A few minutes later two men walked out to the waiting cab. They looked inside, glanced up and down the sidewalk; then they spoke questioningly to the driver, who shrugged his shoulders. At that moment a crowded streetcar was passing by, filled largely with native dock workers in blue overalls. Inside it the dim lights flickered, the standees swayed. Rounding the corner and clanging its bell, it started up the hill past the Café d'Eckmühl-Noiseux where the awnings flapped in the evening breeze, past the Bar Métropole with its radio that roared, past the Café de France, shining with mirrors and brass. Noisily it pushed along, cleaving a passage through the crowd that filled the street, it scraped around another corner, and began the slow ascent of the Avenue Galliéni. Below, the harbor lights came into view and were distorted in the gently moving water. Then the shabbier buildings loomed, the streets were dimmer. At the edge of the Arab quarter the car, still loaded with people, made a wide U-turn and stopped; it was the end of the line.

—PAUL BOWLES, *The Sheltering Sky*

(Rushing to return to their Cornwall estate, Manderley, which the mysterious housekeeper, Mrs. Danvers, has suddenly left, the de Winters find it, and the specter of Rebecca, in flames.)
"Maxim," I said. "Maxim, what is it?"

He drove faster, much faster. We topped the hill before us and saw Lanyon lying in a hollow at our feet. There to the left of us was the silver streak of the river, widening to the estuary at Kerrith six miles away. The road to Manderley lay ahead. There was no moon. The sky above our heads was inky black. But the sky on the horizon was not dark at all. It was shot with crimson, like a splash of blood. And the ashes blew towards us with the salt wind from the sea.

—DAPHNE DU MAURIER, *Rebecca*

Paradise Lost 🌿
Things will never be the same.

(Wandering out into the snow, Gerald Crich has frozen to death in the Alps. Ursula tries to understand her husband's obsession with his dead friend.)

"Did you need Gerald?" she asked one evening.

"Yes," he said.

"Aren't I enough for you?" she asked.

"No," he said. "You are enough for me, as far as a woman is concerned. You are all women to me. But I wanted a man friend, as eternal as you and I are eternal."

"Why aren't I enough?" she said. "You are enough for me. I don't want anybody else but you. Why isn't it the same with you?"

"Having you, I can live all my life without anybody else, any other sheer intimacy. But to make it complete, really happy, I wanted eternal union with a man too: another kind of love," he said.

"I don't believe it," she said. "It's an obstinacy, a theory, a perversity."

"Well—" he said.

"You can't have two kinds of love. Why should you!"

"It seems as if I can't," he said. "Yet I wanted it."

"You can't have it, because it's false, impossible," she said.

"I don't believe that," he answered.

—D. H. LAWRENCE, *Women in Love*

(Abandoned by fortune-hunting Morris Townsend because of her threatened disinheritance, the heiress Catherine Sloper has the grim satisfaction of rejecting him when he returns at the urging of her aunt after the death of Catherine's father.)

"That was a precious plan of yours!" said Morris, clapping on his hat.

"Is she so hard?" asked Mrs. Penniman.

"She doesn't care a button for me—with her confounded little dry manner."

"Was it very dry?" pursued Mrs. Penniman, with solicitude.

Morris took no notice of her question; he stood musing an instant, with his hat on. "But why the deuce, then, would she never marry?"

"Yes—why indeed?" sighed Mrs. Penniman. And then, as if from a sense of the inadequacy of this explanation, "But you will not despair—you will come back?"

"Come back? Damnation!" And Morris Townsend strode out of the house, leaving Mrs. Penniman staring.

Catherine, meanwhile, in the parlor, picking up her morsel of fancy-work, had seated herself with it again—for life, as it were.

—HENRY JAMES, *Washington Square*

(Lady Brett Ashley, who, while waiting for her divorce, had fallen unhappily in love with Jake Barnes, an American correspondent emasculated by a war wound, is leaving Madrid to return to the man she was planning to marry once she was free.)
Down-stairs we came out through the first-floor dining-room to the street. A waiter went for a taxi. It was hot and bright. Up the street was a little square with trees and grass where there were taxis parked. A taxi came up the street, the waiter hanging out at the side. I tipped him and told the driver where to drive, and got in beside Brett. The driver

started up the street. I settled back. Brett moved close to me. We sat close against each other. I put my arm around her and she rested against me comfortably. It was very hot and bright, and the houses looked sharply white. We turned out onto the Gran Via.

"Oh, Jake," Brett said, "we could have had such a damned good time together."

Ahead was a mounted policeman in khaki directing traffic. He raised his baton. The car slowed suddenly pressing Brett against me.

"Yes," I said. "Isn't it pretty to think so?"

—ERNEST HEMINGWAY, *The Sun Also Rises*

(Maria tearfully tells Porgy that Bess has been taken off to Savannah in Porgy's absence, in an ending with none of the hope of the Gershwin opera, Porgy and Bess.)

Deep sobs stopped Maria's voice. For a while she sat there, her face buried in her hands. But Porgy had nothing to say. When she finally raised her head and looked at him, she was surprised at what she saw.

The keen autumn sun flooded boldly through the entrance and bathed the drooping form of the goat, the ridiculous wagon, and the bent figure of the man in hard, satirical radiance. In its revealing light, Maria saw that Porgy was an old man. The early tension that had characterized him, the mellow mood that he had known for one eventful summer, both had gone; and in their place she saw a face that sagged wearily, and the eyes of age lit only by a faint reminiscent glow from suns and moons that had looked into them, and had already dropped down the west.

She looked until she could bear the sight no longer; then she stumbled into her shop and closed the door, leaving Porgy and the goat alone in an irony of morning sunlight.

—Du Bose Heyward, *Porgy*

And as I sat there brooding on the old, unknown world, I thought of Gatsby's wonder when he first picked out the green light at the end of Daisy's dock. He had come a long way to this blue lawn, and his dream must have seemed so close that he could hardly fail to grasp it. He did not know that it was already behind him, somewhere back in that vast obscurity beyond the city, where the dark fields of the republic rolled on under the night.

Gatsby believed in the green light, the orgiastic future that year by year recedes before us. It eluded us then, but that's no matter—tomorrow we will run faster, stretch out our arms farther. . . . And one fine morning—

So we beat on, boats against the current, borne back ceaselessly into the past.

—F. Scott Fitzgerald, *The Great Gatsby*

21 ❧ THE DEAD END

s birth is a natural beginning to a novel, death is a natural end. Whether it is the hero who dies or a person beloved or hated by the hero, this last action is often the climactic event of the book. I use the term "climax" not in the theatrical sense, where it is an action by the protagonist that can occur near the middle of the play—for example, Hamlet's killing of Polonius, after which Hamlet moves inexorably toward the unhappy resolution of the play—but as that point toward which the story has been building, and where the action really ends.

In many, perhaps most, cases the death pivotal to the plot occurs in the penultimate chapter, the last being saved to show the effect that the event has on the major character or characters. This chapter is an anticlimax or what might be more accurately called a postclimax: the forward movement of the story has been halted at the point of highest tension, and the last chapter is only a period of cooling down and reflection. Thus John Galsworthy describes the death of the honest but pitiable Soames Forsyte in the next-to-last chapter of *Swan Song*, the final book of *The Forsyte Saga*. His daughter, Fleur, waits with him for the doctor:

> "Gradman is here, darling, and Mother, and Aunt Winifred, and Kit and Michael. Is there anyone you would like to see?"
>
> His lips shaped: "No—you!"
>
> "I am here all the time." Again she felt the tremor from his fingers, saw his lips whispering:
>
> "That's all."
>
> And suddenly, his eyes went out. There was nothing there! For some time longer he breathed, but before "that fellow" came, he had lost hold—was gone.

Galsworthy uses the last chapter to establish the ultimate effect of the death. Through the eyes of Soames's son-in-law, Michael Mont, we see that the marriage of Michael and Fleur will survive Soames's death and Fleur's infidelity.

Killing off a character as strong as Soames is not an easy undertaking, as Sir Arthur Conan Doyle found when he attempted to do away with Sherlock Holmes. The outcry from readers was so great that, much to the annoyance of his creator, the character had to be brought back in another book. There was to be no such miraculous reappearance for Soames once Galsworthy had decided on his death. Nearing the completion of *Swan Song*, Galsworthy wrote to a friend that he thought Soames would "survive" the book, but four months later he confided that he had finished the novel and "after all 'Le Roi est mort'—" It was a not insignificant decision for Galsworthy or his readers.

The Harder They Fall 🦅
Deaths of the great and near-great.

He continued to murmur, to move his hands a little, and Magdalena thought he was trying to ask for something, or to tell them something. But in reality the Bishop was not there at all; he was standing in a tip-tilted green field among his native mountains, and he was trying to give consolation to a young man who was being torn in two before his eyes by the desire to go and the necessity to stay. He was trying to forge a new Will in that devout and exhausted priest; and the time was short, for the *diligence* for Paris was already rumbling down the mountain gorge.

When the Cathedral bell tolled just after dark, the Mexican population of Santa Fé fell upon their knees, and all American Catholics as well. Many others who did not kneel prayed in their hearts. Eusabio and the Tesuque boys went quietly away to tell their people; and the next morning the old Archbishop lay before the high altar in the church he had built.

—WILLA CATHER, *Death Comes for the Archbishop*

The second page of a letter from John Galsworthy to Harley Granville-Barker, August 12, 1927, revealing that the author had "killed" his character, Soames Forsyte, in the final book of *The Forsyte Saga*: "after all 'Le Roi est mort—'" *(Houghton Library, Harvard University, bMS Eng 1020 [39])*

(Libanius has been forbidden by the Emperor to publish Julian's biography.)

I have been reading Plotinus all evening. He has the power to soothe me; and I find his sadness curiously comforting. Even when he writes: "Life here with the things of earth is a sinking, a defeat, a failing of the wing." The wing has indeed failed. One sinks. Defeat is certain. Even as I write these lines, the lamp wick sputters to an end, and the pool of light in which I sit contracts. Soon the room will be dark. One has always feared that death would be like this. But what else is there? With Julian, the light went, and now nothing remains but to let the darkness come, and hope for a new sun and another day, born of time's mystery and man's love of light.

—GORE VIDAL, *Julian*

(From Suetonius: The Lives of the Caesars: *Book One.)*

. . . As Caesar exclaimed: "Then this is violence!" one of the Cascas, standing at his side, plunged a dagger into him, just below the throat. Caesar caught hold of Casca's arm and ran his pen through it; but as he tried to rise to his feet he was held down by another stab. When he saw that he was surrounded on all sides by drawn daggers, he wrapped his head in his robe at the same time drawing its folds about his feet with his left hand so that when he fell the lower part of his body would be decorously covered.

In this manner then he was stabbed twenty-three times. He said no word, merely groaned at the first stroke, though certain writers have said that when Marcus Brutus fell upon him he said in Greek, "You, too, my son!"

All the conspirators took themselves off and left him lying there dead for some time. Finally three common slaves put him on a litter and carried him home, one arm hanging down over the side.

Antistius the physician said that of all those wounds only the second one in the breast would have proved fatal.

—THORNTON WILDER, *The Ides of March*

(General Simón Bolívar, forced from power, realizes that he is dying.)
"Damn it," he sighed. "How will I ever get out of this labyrinth!"

He examined the room with the clairvoyance of his last days, and for the first time he saw the truth: the final borrowed bed, the pitiful dressing table whose clouded, patient mirror would not reflect his image again, the chipped porcelain washbasin with the water and towel and soap meant for other hands, the heartless speed of the octagonal clock racing toward the ineluctable appointment at seven minutes past one on his final afternoon of December 17. Then he crossed his arms over his chest and began to listen to the radiant voices of the slaves singing the six o'clock *Salve* in the mills, and through the window he saw the diamond of Venus in the sky that was dying forever, the eternal snows, the new vine whose yellow bellflowers he would not see bloom on the following Saturday in the house closed in mourning, the final brilliance of life that would never, through all eternity, be repeated again.

—Gabriel García Márquez,
The General in His Labyrinth,
trans. Edith Grossman

Murder Most Foul 🌱
Death comes violently.

(An Autobahn patrolman finds James Bond and his new bride, whose Lancia has crashed after having been shot at from a Maserati.) Bond turned towards Tracy. She was lying forward with her face buried in the ruins of the steering-wheel. Her pink handkerchief had come off and the bell of golden hair hung down and hid her face. Bond put his arm round her shoulders, across which the dark patches had begun to flower.

He pressed her against him. He looked up at the young man and smiled his reassurance.

"It's all right," he said in a clear voice as if explaining something to a child. "It's quite all right. She's having a rest. We'll be going on soon. There's no hurry. You see"—Bond's head sank down against hers and he whispered into her hair—"you see, we've got all the time in the world."

The young patrolman took a last scared look at the motionless couple, hurried over to his motor-cycle, picked up the hand-microphone and began talking urgently to the rescue headquarters.

—Ian Fleming, *On Her Majesty's Secret Service*

(The Captain goes to the room of his wife, whom he suspects of infidelity, to find crouching at the side of the bed a soldier who had been stealing into her room as she slept.)
The soldier did not have time to rise from his squatting position. He blinked at the light and there was no fear in his face; his expression was one of dazed annoyance, as if he had been inexcusably disturbed. The Captain was a good marksman, and although he shot twice only one raw hole was left in the center of the soldier's chest.

The reports from the pistol aroused Leonora and she sat up in bed. As yet she was still only half-awake, and she stared about her as though witnessing some scene in a play, some tragedy that was gruesome but not necessary to believe. Almost immediately Major Langdon knocked on the back door and then hurried up the stairs wearing slippers and a dressing-gown. The Captain had slumped against the wall. In his queer, coarse wrapper he resembled a broken and dissipated monk. Even in death the body of the soldier still had the look of warm, animal comfort. His grave face was unchanged, and his sun-browned hands lay palms upward on the carpet as though in sleep.

—CARSON MCCULLERS, *Reflections in a Golden Eye*

(The ship's officer, Ryuji, is to be murdered by a group of young boys for deserting the sea to live on land and to marry the mother of one of them, Noboru.)
. . . Surging out of the splendor of the sea, death had swept down on him like a stormy bank of clouds. A vision of death

now eternally beyond his reach, majestic, acclaimed, heroic death unfurled its rapture across his brain. And if the world had been provided for just this radiant death, then why shouldn't the world also perish for it!

Waves, as tepid as blood, inside an atoll. The tropical sun blaring across the sky like the call of a brass trumpet. The many-colored sea. Sharks. . . .

Another step or two and Ryuji would have regretted it.

"Here's your tea," Noboru offered from behind him, thrusting a dark-brown plastic cup near Ryuji's cheek. Absently, Ryuji took it. He noticed Noboru's hand trembling slightly, probably from the cold.

Still immersed in his dream, he drank down the tepid tea. It tasted bitter. Glory, as anyone knows, is bitter stuff.

—YUKIO MISHIMA,
The Sailor Who Fell from Grace with the Sea,
trans. John Nathan

(Fighting in the Loyalist Army in the Spanish Civil War, Robert Jordan lies wounded, waiting with the last of his strength to kill a Fascist leader.)

As the officer came trotting now on the trail of the horses of the band he would pass twenty yards below where Robert Jordan lay. At that distance there would be no problem. The officer was Lieutenant Berrendo. He had come up from La Granja when they had been ordered up after the first report of the attack on the lower post. They had ridden hard and had then had to swing back, because the bridge had been blown, to cross the gorge high above and come around through the timber. Their horses were wet and blown and they had to be urged into the trot.

Lieutenant Berrendo, watching the trail, came riding up, his thin face serious and grave. His submachine gun lay across his saddle in the crook of his left arm. Robert Jordan lay behind the tree, holding onto himself very carefully and delicately to keep his hands steady. He was waiting until the officer reached the sunlit place where the first trees of the pine forest joined the green slope of the meadow. He could feel his heart beating against the pine needle floor of the forest.

—ERNEST HEMINGWAY, *For Whom the Bell Tolls*

(Joseph K., without being told the crime of which he has been accused, is interrogated, released, then taken into custody, marched to a quarry, and executed.)
With a flicker as of a light going up, the casements of a window there suddenly flew open; a human figure, faint and insubstantial at that distance and that height, leaned abruptly far forward and stretched both arms still farther. Who was it? A friend? A good man? Someone who sympathized? Someone who wanted to help? Was it one person only? Or was it mankind? Was help at hand? Were there arguments in his favor that had been overlooked? Of course there must be. Logic is doubtless unshakable, but it cannot withstand a man who wants to go on living. Where was the Judge whom he had never seen? Where was the High Court, to which he

had never penetrated? He raised his hands and spread out all his fingers.

But the hands of one of the partners were already at K.'s throat, while the other thrust the knife deep into his heart and turned it there twice. With failing eyes K. could still see the two of them immediately before him, cheek leaning against cheek, watching the final act. "Like a dog!" he said; it was as if the shame of it must outlive him.

—FRANZ KAFKA, *The Trial*,
trans. Willa and Edward Muir,
revised by E. M. Butler

Suicidal Tendencies 🎐
The hero writes his own ending.

(As the effects of worldwide atomic bombing reach Australia, Moira Davidson faces a slow radioactive death while Dwight Towers takes his life in the American submarine he will sink.)

Presently she could see the submarine no longer; it had vanished in the mist. She looked at her little wrist watch; it showed one minute past ten. Her childhood religion came back to her in those last minutes; one ought to do something about that, she thought. A little alcoholically she murmured the Lord's Prayer.

Then she took out the red carton from her bag, and opened the vial, and held the tablets in her hand. Another spasm shook her, and she smiled faintly. "Foxed you this time," she said.

She took the cork out of the bottle. It was ten past ten. She said earnestly, "Dwight, if you're on your way already, wait for me."

Then she put the tablets in her mouth and swallowed them down with a mouthful of brandy, sitting behind the wheel of her big car.

—NEVIL SHUTE, *On the Beach*

He raised his eyes, looked through the kitchen window, saw the immense Greek coping of the library, the huge words cut in granite, Harry Elkins Widener Library, then beyond it the slate roof of Boylston Hall, and farther still the gray wooden steeple of the Unitarian Church. There was a faint smell of coffee coming from the professor's apartment, it mixed oddly with the not unpleasant smell of the gas, he was aware that he was hungry.

But also he was sleepy, it would be very easy to fall asleep. By this time, Jones would have got back to the shabby little house in Reservoir Street—the grave at Mount Auburn would have been filled—the khaki-clad messenger was sitting in a subway train on his way to Beacon Hill. And Gerta— would she be there? would she come? was she standing there at her open window, with an apple in her hand, looking down over the roofs to the morning sunlight flashing on the Charles River Basin? wearing the white Russian blouse?

Half past nine. The professor's clock sent its soft *tyang* through the walls. He closed his eyes.

—CONRAD AIKEN, *King Coffin*

This balcony clings to the living cliff. I see a walk beyond it, threading the crag. That will do well. If I go from here, it might be said that Lykomedes murdered me. It would be discourteous to shame my host. But there is only Akamas left to ask my blood-price; and he, though he is half Cretan, knows well enough how the Erechthids die.

Surely goats made this track. That boy, Achilles, might scramble here for a dare. No place, this, for a dragging foot; but all the better. It will seem like mischance, except to those who know.

The tide comes in. A swelling sea, calm, strong and shining. To swim under the moon, onward and onward, plunging with the dolphins, singing . . . To leap with the wind in my hair . . .

—MARY RENAULT, *The Bull from the Sea*

That evening the swarm of helicopters that came buzzing across the Hog's Back was a dark cloud ten kilometres long. The description of last night's orgy of atonement had been in all the papers.

"Savage!" called the first arrivals, as they alighted from their machine. "Mr. Savage!"

There was no answer.

The door of the lighthouse was ajar. They pushed it open and walked into a shuttered twilight. Through an archway on the further side of the room they could see the bottom of the staircase that led up to the higher floors. Just under the crown of the arch dangled a pair of feet.

"Mr. Savage!"

Slowly, very slowly, like two unhurried compass needles, the feet turned towards the right; north, north-east, east, south-east, south, south-south-west; then paused, and, after a few seconds, turned as unhurriedly back towards the left. South-south-west, south, south-east, east. . . .

—ALDOUS HUXLEY, *Brave New World*

Go Gently 🦋
Death as letting go.

(Adam's wise Chinese servant, Lee, urges the dying man to forgive his son, Caleb, for causing the death of his brother, Aron, who ran away to the war. He gives his blessing with a Hebrew word meaning "thou mayest.")

A terrible brightness shone in Adam's eyes and he closed them and kept them closed. A wrinkle formed between his brows.

Lee said, "Help him, Adam—help him. Give him his chance. Let him be free. That's all a man has over the beasts. Free him! Bless him!"

The whole bed seemed to shake under the concentration. Adam's breath came quick with his effort and then, slowly, his right hand lifted—lifted an inch and then fell back.

Lee's face was haggard. He moved to the head of the bed and wiped the sick man's damp face with the edge of the sheet. He looked down at the closed eyes. Lee whispered, "Thank you, Adam—thank you, my friend. Can you move your lips? Make your lips form his name."

Adam looked up with sick weariness. His lips parted and
failed and tried again. Then his lungs filled. He expelled the
air and his lips combed the rushing sigh. His whispered word
seemed to hang in the air:

"*Timshel!*"

His eyes closed and he slept.

—JOHN STEINBECK, *East of Eden*

*(Philip Ashley, suspecting that the woman who married his cousin
has poisoned both her late husband and himself, does not warn her
about an unfinished bridge as she goes for a walk in the garden.)*
I came to the edge of the wall above the sunken garden and
saw where the men had started work upon the bridge. Part
of the bridge still remained and hung suspended, grotesque
and horrible, like a swinging ladder. The rest had fallen to
the depths below.

I climbed down to where she lay amongst the timber and
the stones. I took her hands and held them. They were
cold.

"Rachel," I said to her, and "Rachel" once again.

The dogs began barking up above, and louder still came
the sound of the clanging bell. She opened her eyes and
looked at me. At first, I think, in pain. Then in bewilderment. Then finally, so I thought, in recognition. Yet I was in
error, even then. She called me Ambrose. I went on holding
her hands until she died.

They used to hang men at Four Turnings in the old days. Not any more, though.

—DAPHNE DU MAURIER, My Cousin Rachel

(George Apley writes to his son John about his own funeral arrangements and the boy's return and entrance into Boston society.)
But I am getting very far afield. I am speaking very prosily, out of sheer joy at having you come back. We can talk about all these matters together much more sensibly than I can ever put them down on paper. My mind and my heart are both too full for writing. I repeat I always knew that you had the right stuff in you and now we will have a chance to get to know each other. What I want particularly is to have a great many small men's dinners. There is so much to say. There is so much to talk about. God bless you. . . .

George Apley died in his own house on Beacon Street on the thirteenth of December, 1933, two weeks after John Apley returned to Boston.

—JOHN MARQUAND, The Late George Apley

From his expression and the pitch of his voice, the boy is shouting into a fierce wind blowing from his father's direction. "Don't die, Dad, don't!" he cries, then sits back with that question still on his face, and his dark wet eyes shining like stars of a sort. Harry shouldn't leave the question hanging like that, the boy depends on him.

"Well, Nelson," he says, "all I can tell you is, it isn't so bad." Rabbit thinks he should maybe say more, the kid looks wildly expectant, but enough. Maybe. Enough.

—JOHN UPDIKE, *Rabbit at Rest*

Last Words 🦋
A final good-bye to the dead.

Coming thus near to the summit of one of the high mountains of the Jura, in the middle of the night, in that little cave magnificently illuminated with countless candles, a score of priests celebrated the Office of the Dead. All the inhabitants of the little mountain villages, through which the procession passed, had followed it, drawn by the singularity of this strange ceremony.

Mathilde appeared in their midst in a flowing garb of mourning, and, at the end of the service, had several thousands of five franc pieces scattered among them.

Left alone with Fouqué, she insisted upon burying her lover's head with her own hands. Fouqué almost went mad with grief.

By Mathilde's orders, this savage grot was adorned with marbles sculptured at great cost, in Italy.

Madame de Rênal was faithful to her promise. She did not seek in any way to take her own life; but, three days after Julien, died while embracing her children.

—STENDHAL, *The Red and the Black,*
trans. C. K. Scott Moncrieff

(Sammler speaks to the body of his nephew Elya, which is lying on a stretcher in the hospital morgue.)

Sammler in a mental whisper said, "Well, Elya. Well, well, Elya." And then in the same way he said, "Remember, God, the soul of Elya Gruner, who, as willingly as possible and as well as he was able, and even to an intolerable point, and even in suffocation and even as death was coming was eager, even childishly perhaps (may I be forgiven for this), even with a certain servility, to do what was required of him. At his best this man was much kinder than at my very best I have ever been or could ever be. He was aware that he must meet, and he did meet—through all the confusion and degraded clowning of this life through which we are speeding—he did meet the terms of his contract. The terms which, in his inmost heart, each man knows. As I know mine. As all know. For that is the truth of it—that we all know, God, that we know, that we know, we know, we know."

—SAUL BELLOW, *Mr. Sammler's Planet*

He saw that all the conditions of life had conspired to keep them apart; since his very detachment from the external influences which swayed her had increased his spiritual fastidiousness, and made it more difficult for him to live and love uncritically. But at least he *had* loved her—had been willing to stake his future on his faith in her—and if the moment had been fated to pass from them before they could seize it, he saw now that, for both, it had been saved whole out of the ruin of their lives.

It was this moment of love, this fleeting victory over themselves, which had kept them from atrophy and extinction; which, in her, had reached out to him in every struggle against the influence of her surroundings, and in him, had kept alive the faith that now drew him penitent and reconciled to her side.

He knelt by the bed and bent over her, draining their last moment to its lees; and in the silence there passed between them the word which made all clear.

—EDITH WHARTON, *The House of Mirth*

(Hazel Motes's landlady, because she herself is losing her sight, doesn't realize that her blinded tenant is dead.)
She had never observed his face more composed and she grabbed his hand and held it to her heart. It was resistless and dry. The outline of a skull was plain under his skin and the deep burned eye sockets seemed to lead into the dark tunnel where he had disappeared. She leaned closer and closer to his face, looking deep into them, trying to see how she had been cheated or what had cheated her, but she couldn't see anything. She shut her eyes and saw the pin point of light but so far away that she could not hold it steady in her mind. She felt as if she were blocked at the entrance of something. She sat staring with her eyes shut, into his eyes, and felt as if she had finally got to the beginning of something she couldn't begin, and she saw him moving farther and farther away, farther and farther into the darkness until he was the pin point of light.

—FLANNERY O'CONNOR, *Wise Blood*

Postmortem 🦋

The survivors struggle with their memories.

(Preceding a mob from the ranch on which they are workers, George finds and kills his companion, the simpleminded Lennie, who has accidentally murdered the wife of the boss's son, Curley.)
Slim came directly to George and sat down beside him, sat very close to him. "Never you mind," said Slim. "A guy got to sometimes."

But Carlson was standing over George. "How'd you do it?" he asked.

"I just done it," George said tiredly.

"Did he have my gun?"

"Yeah. He had your gun."

"An' you got it away from him and you took it an' you killed him?"

"Yeah. Tha's how." George's voice was almost a whisper. He looked steadily at his right hand that had held the gun.

Slim twitched George's elbow. "Come on, George. Me an' you'll go in an' get a drink."

George let himself be helped to his feet. "Yeah, a drink."

Slim said, "You hadda, George. I swear you hadda. Come on with me." He led George into the entrance of the trail and up toward the highway.

Curley and Carlson looked after them. And Carlson said, "Now what the hell ya suppose is eatin' them two guys?"

—JOHN STEINBECK, *Of Mice and Men*

(Mrs. Hale relates how Ethan and Mattie, crippled for life from a lovers' suicide attempt, must depend on Ethan's harping wife to care for them.)

She took off her spectacles again, leaned toward me across the bead-work table-cover, and went on with lowered voice: "There was one day, about a week after the accident, when they all thought Mattie couldn't live. Well, I say it's a pity she *did*. I said it right out to our minister once, and he was shocked at me. Only he wasn't with me that morning when she first came to . . . And I say, if she'd ha' died, Ethan might ha' lived; and the way they are now, I don't see's there's much difference between the Fromes up at the farm and the Fromes down in the graveyard; 'cept that down there they're all quiet, and the women have got to hold their tongues."

—EDITH WHARTON, *Ethan Frome*

When the short funeral procession started, Mary and the infirm Fossette (sole relic of the connection between the Baines family and Paris) were left alone in the house. The tearful servant prepared the dog's dinner and laid it before her in the customary soup-plate in the customary corner. Fossette sniffed at it, and then walked away and lay down with a dog's sigh in front of the kitchen fire. She had been deranged in her habits that day; she was conscious of neglect, due to events which passed her comprehension. And she did not like it. She was hurt, and her appetite was hurt.

However, after a few minutes, she began to reconsider the matter. She glanced at the soup-plate, and, on the chance that it might after all contain something worth inspection, she awkwardly balanced herself on her old legs and went to it again.

—ARNOLD BENNETT, The Old Wives' Tale

(Don Fabrizio's spinster daughter, Concetta, whose only love, Tancredi, has died, disposes of her dead father's possessions, including his stuffed dog.)

Still she could feel nothing; the inner emptiness was complete; but she did sense an unpleasant atmosphere exhaling from the heap of furs. That was to-day's distress: even poor Bendicò was hinting at bitter memories. She rang the bell. "Annetta," she said, "This dog has really become too moth-eaten and dusty. Take it out and throw it away."

As the carcass was dragged off, the glass eyes stared at her with the humble reproach of things that are thrown away, got rid of. A few minutes later what remained of Bendicò was flung into a corner of the courtyard visited every day by the dustman. During the flight down from the window its form recomposed itself for an instant; in the air there seemed to be dancing a quadruped with long whiskers, its right foreleg raised in imprecation. Then all found peace in a heap of livid dust.

—GIUSEPPE DI LAMPEDUSA, The Leopard,
trans. Archibald Colquhoun

22 ❦ IRONY—WITH A TWIST, PLEASE

What extraordinary power the novelist holds over us as he or she brings the story to a close! The author can make us laugh or cry, can inspire us with hope or make us ache with despair. Or toy with us, telling us one thing when really something very different is meant, and playing with our emotions so that we react first one way then another. The novelist can, in other words, choose to give the ending an ironic twist.

We should know better. If we were alert, we would see that early in the story we are being set up by being given little clues that will eventually lead to the "trick" ending. But if the novelist is doing the job cleverly, we will accept these clues for what they seem to be: details of character or plot that only take on a greater meaning when we view the whole story with the benefit of that seventh sense, hindsight. At that point, irony delivers an emotional whammy.

The dramatic power inherent in this effect is the reason irony is such a popular ending with playwrights and television and screenwriters, where it is commonly called the "twist." A very contemporary ending, it's as old as the ancient Greeks, from whom it originated. In fact, one form of irony, in which a feigned innocent statement is used to prove an opponent wrong, is called Socratic irony.

Scholars have identified many different ironic forms: verbal, including the use of sarcasm, in which the dialogue contains the contradiction; dramatic, which is brought about by a situation or fateful series of events that lead to the exact opposite result from that expected by the protagonist and which gives us our greatest tragedies; comic, which hurts us even as we laugh; the irony of character, in which the character himself gives the lie to our, and sometimes his, expectations, an un-unveiled Tartuffe; and many others, such as symbolic, recurring, malignant, benevolent, and subconscious irony. Although they function somewhat differently, all are based on a single principle: deception. And the deceiver is the author, pretending one thing and meaning its opposite, acting on the characters as it sometimes seems Fate acts on us in real life, unreasonably, heartlessly, and with supreme fickleness.

Our reaction to the ironic ending is twofold: intellectually we recognize that what we see is not what it is purported to be, and we appreciate the cleverness with which we have been taken in; and emotionally we feel some hurt, or at least discomfort, in perceiving the truth. We get the joke, but we do not wholly like it. It is like black comedy where, in the middle of a laugh, we gasp in horror at its implications.

The author can achieve a similar emotional impact through ironic understatement, that is, by seemingly leaving out what is most important. The author ends the book with a coolness and distance, and we as readers, realizing what has been left unsaid, fill in the blanks. So John Fowles's narrator in *The Collector*, having slowly killed the young woman he has kept imprisoned in a room in his house, buries the body and considers preparing the room for a new victim, concluding: "But it is still just an idea. I only put the stove down there today because the room needs drying out anyway." What seems an innocent observation by the "collector" makes our skin crawl as we realize the author's implication.

How Ironic! ❦

The author has a last wry smile at our expense.

(Madame Bovary is dead from arsenic obtained from the pharmacist; her husband, Charles, dies disillusioned and in poverty.)
When everything was sold, there remained twelve francs and fifteen centimes—enough to pay Mademoiselle Bovary's coach fare to her grandmother's. The old lady died the same year; and since Monsieur Rouault was now paralyzed, it was an aunt who took charge of her. She is poor, and sends her to work for her living in a cotton mill.

Since Bovary's death, three doctors have succeeded one another in Yonville, and not one of them has gained a foothold, so rapidly and so utterly has Homais routed them. The devil himself doesn't have a greater following than the pharmacist: the authorities treat him considerately, and public opinion is on his side.

He has just been awarded the cross of the Legion of Honor.

—GUSTAVE FLAUBERT, *Madame Bovary*, trans. Francis Steegmuller

The church thundered with the triumphant hallelujah, and in a sacred silence Elmer prayed:

"O Lord, thou hast stooped from thy mighty throne and rescued thy servant from the assault of the mercenaries of Satan! Mostly we thank thee because thus we can go on doing thy work, and thine alone! Not less but more zealously shall we seek utter purity and the prayer-life, and rejoice in freedom from all temptations!"

He turned to include the choir, and for the first time he saw that there was a new singer, a girl with charming ankles and lively eyes, with whom he would certainly have to become well acquainted. But the thought was so swift that it did not interrupt the pæan of his prayer:

"Let me count this day, Lord, as the beginning of a new and more vigorous life, as the beginning of a crusade for complete morality and the domination of the Christian church through all the land. Dear Lord, thy work is but begun! We shall yet make these United States a moral nation!"

—SINCLAIR LEWIS, *Elmer Gantry*

(Karen Holmes is leaving Hawaii for home, after Pearl Harbor and her extramarital love affair with Sergeant Milton Warden.)
She took the six flower leis off over her head and dropped them over the side. This was as good a place to drop them over as any. Diamond Head, Koko Head, Makapuu Head. Perhaps Koko Head was the best place, really. The six leis fell together and the wind blew them back against the side of the ship and out of sight and she did not see them light on the water.

"Mother," her son said from behind her. "I'm hungry. When do we eat on this old boat?"

"Pretty soon now," she said.

"Mother, do you think the war will last long enough so I can graduate from the Point and be in it? Jerry Wilcox said it wouldnt."

"No," she said, "I dont think it'll last that long."

"Well, gee whiz, mother," her son said, "I want to be in it."

"Well, cheer up," Karen said, "and dont let it worry you. You may miss this one, but you'll be just the right age for the next one."

"You really think so, mother?" her son said anxiously.

—JAMES JONES, *From Here to Eternity*

(The scheming Bel-Ami has just married the daughter of his lover, while another mistress, Mme. de Marelle, has intimated that their affair will continue as before.)
When they reached the threshold he saw a crowd gathered outside, come to gaze at him, Georges du Roy. The people

of Paris envied him. Raising his eyes, he saw beyond the
Place de la Concorde, the chamber of deputies, and it
seemed to him that it was only a stone's throw from the por-
tico of the Madeleine to that of the Palais Bourbon.

Leisurely they descended the steps between two rows of
spectators, but Georges did not see them; his thoughts had
returned to the past, and before his eyes, dazzled by the
bright sunlight, floated the image of Mme. de Marelle,
rearranging the curly locks upon her temples before the
mirror in their apartments.

—GUY DE MAUPASSANT, *Bel-Ami*

*(James Bray, an English colonial administrator who had been
expelled from his post in Africa ten years before for supporting local
nationalist leaders, returns and is killed.)*
No one could say for certain whether, when Bray was killed
on the way to the capital, he was going to Mweta or to buy
arms for Shinza. To some, as his friend Dando had predicted,
he was a martyr to savages; to others, one of those madmen
like Geoffrey Bing or Conor Cruise O'Brien who had only
got what he deserved. In a number devoted to "The Decline
of Liberalism" in an English monthly journal he was dis-
cussed as an interesting case in point: a man who had "passed
over from the scepticism and resignation of empirical liberalism to become one of those who are so haunted by the stu-
pidities and evils in human affairs that they are prepared to
accept apocalyptic solutions, wade through blood if need be,
to bring real change."

Hjalmar Wentz also put together Bray's box of papers and gave them over to Dando, who might know what to do with them. Eventually they must have reached the hands of Mweta. He, apparently, chose to believe that Bray was a conciliator; a year later he published a blueprint for the country's new education scheme, the Bray Report.

—NADINE GORDIMER, *A Guest of Honour*

(Captain Chris Baldry is a war victim of amnesia who has resumed a relationship with an innkeeper's daughter because he cannot remember his wife, Kitty. His cousin Jenny watches as he is told the truth by the woman, who sacrifices their happiness for Kitty's.)
. . . He wore a dreadful decent smile; I knew how his voice would resolutely lift in greeting us. He walked not loose limbed like a boy, as he had done that very afternoon, but with the soldier's hard tread upon the heel. It recalled to me that, bad as we were, we were yet not the worst circumstance of his return. When we had lifted the yoke of our embraces from his shoulders he would go back to that flooded trench in Flanders under that sky more full of flying death than clouds, to that No Man's Land where bullets fall like rain on the rotting faces of the dead. . . .

"Jenny, aren't they there?"

"They're both there."

"Is he coming back?"

"He's coming back."

"Jenny, Jenny! How does he look?"

"Oh. . . ." How could I say it? "Every inch a soldier."

She crept behind me to the window, peered over my shoulder and saw.

I heard her suck her breath with satisfaction. "He's cured!" she whispered slowly. "He's cured!"

—REBECCA WEST, *The Return of the Soldier*

That's an Understatement! 🦋
The silence speaks volumes.

The room's cleaned out now and good as new.

I shall put what she wrote and her hair up in the loft in the deed-box which will not be opened till my death, so I don't expect for forty or fifty years. I have not made up my mind about Marian (another M! I heard the supervisor call her name), this time it won't be love, it would just be for the interest of the thing and to compare them and also the other thing, which as I say I would like to go into in more detail and I could teach her how. And the clothes would fit. Of course I would make it clear from the start who's boss and what I expect.

But it is still just an idea. I only put the stove down there today because the room needs drying out anyway.

—JOHN FOWLES, *The Collector*

(*John Dowell is aware that Edward Ashburnham is about to commit suicide, Ashburnham having just received a telegram from the young girl he loves, whom Leonora, his wife, has connived to banish to India.*)

Then he put two fingers into the waistcoat pocket of his grey, frieze suit; they came out with a little neat penknife—quite a small penknife. He said to me:

"You might just take that wire to Leonora." And he looked at me with a direct, challenging, brow-beating glare. I guess he could see in my eyes that I didn't intend to hinder him. Why should I hinder him?

I didn't think he was wanted in the world, let his confounded tenants, his rifle-associations, his drunkards, reclaimed and unreclaimed, get on as they liked. Not all the hundreds and hundreds of them deserved that that poor devil should go on suffering for their sakes.

When he saw that I did not intend to interfere with him his eyes became soft and almost affectionate. He remarked:

"So long, old man, I must have a bit of a rest, you know."

I didn't know what to say. I wanted to say: "God bless you," for I also am a sentimentalist. But I thought that perhaps that would not be quite English good form, so I trotted off with the telegram to Leonora. She was quite pleased with it.

—FORD MADOX FORD, *The Good Soldier*

. . . I have spoken of a voice telling me things. I was getting to know it better now, to understand what it wanted. It did not use the words that Moran had been taught when he was little and that he in his turn had taught to his little one. So that at first I did not know what it wanted. But in the end I understood this language. I understood it, I understood it, all wrong perhaps. That is not what matters. It told me to write the report. Does this mean I am freer now than I was? I do not know. I shall learn. Then I went back into the house and wrote, It is midnight. The rain is beating on the windows. It was not midnight. It was not raining.

—SAMUEL BECKETT, *Molloy*, trans. Patrick Bowles in collaboration with the author

". . . and the cooking is getting perfectly disgraceful. I spoke to Culyer about it only yesterday. But he won't do anything. I don't know what's the good of the committee. This club isn't half what it used to be. In fact, Wimsey, I'm thinking of resigning."

"Oh, don't do that, Wetheridge. It wouldn't be the same place without you."

"Look at all the disturbance there has been lately. Police and reporters—and then Penberthy blowing his brains out in the library. And the coal's all slate. Only yesterday something exploded like a shell—I assure you, exactly like a shell—in the card-room; and as nearly as possible got me in the eye. I said to Culyer, 'This must *not* occur again.' You may laugh, but I knew a man who was blinded by a thing popping out suddenly like that. These things never happened before the War, and—great heavens! William! Look at this wine! Smell it! *Taste* it! Corked? Yes, I should think it *was* corked! My God! I don't know what's come to this club."

—DOROTHY L. SAYERS, *The Unpleasantness at the Bellona Club*

23 ❧ SURPRISE!

he quintessential surprise ending is the revelation of the murderer in the mystery novel. If the story has been well planned, this surprise will take the reader totally unawares, yet it will be entirely logical and acceptable because of the preparation that has gone before. A track will have been laid and clues given throughout the book, clues that mean little when we first read them but that make absolute sense when the surprise is revealed. "Of course," we say to ourselves, "it was so obvious if only I'd seen."

The same basic rules apply to the surprise ending of a non-mystery novel. Carefully laid clues prepare us for what is to come, and because we accept them as we progress through the book, we accept the author's tricking us at the end. Although the ending appears on the surface to be unexpected, it really *has* been expected all along. When we think about it, two and two *do* make four.

The author has again deceived us, but our reaction to this kind of deception is very different from our response to the ironic ending, which makes us somewhat uncomfortable. With the surprise ending, we are pleased. Pleased that we have been fooled. Pleased with relief from the tension that has been building. Pleased that a solution has appeared as miraculously as the proverbial knight in shining armor.

Yet although the surprise comes magically, it still must make sense to us, based on all we have read previously in the book. If it doesn't, if it is surprise for the sake of surprise, our reaction is not pleasure. It is disbelief and annoyance.

The Hat Trick 🦌
The author pulls out a rabbit.

(Having killed the painter of his portrait, which ages while he doesn't, Dorian Gray stabs the painting, then falls to the floor with a crash and cry.)

Inside, in the servants' part of the house, the half-clad domestics were talking in low whispers to each other. Old Mrs. Leaf was crying and wringing her hands. Francis was as pale as death.

After about a quarter of an hour, he got the coachman and one of the footmen and crept upstairs. They knocked, but there was no reply. They called out. Everything was still. Finally, after vainly trying to force the door, they got on the roof, and dropped down on to the balcony. The windows yielded easily: their bolts were old.

When they entered they found, hanging upon the wall, a splendid portrait of their master as they had last seen him, in all the wonder of his exquisite youth and beauty. Lying on the floor was a dead man, in evening dress, with a knife in his heart. He was withered, wrinkled, and loathsome of visage. It was not till they had examined the rings that they recognised who it was.

—OSCAR WILDE, *The Picture of Dorian Gray*

(The creature, on board ship in the Arctic with the explorer Walton, cries out his remorse to the dead Frankenstein.)
"But soon," he cried, with sad and solemn enthusiasm, "I shall die, and what I now feel be no longer felt. Soon these burning miseries will be extinct. I shall ascend my funeral pile triumphantly, and exult in the agony of the torturing flames. The light of that conflagration will fade away; my ashes will be swept into the sea by the winds. My spirit will sleep in peace; or if it thinks, it will not surely think thus. Farewell."

He sprung from the cabin-window, as he said this, upon the ice-raft which lay close to the vessel. He was soon borne away by the waves and lost in darkness and distance.

—MARY SHELLEY, *Frankenstein*

(Ulysse Mérou returns to Earth with Nova, the beautiful woman he has rescued from Soror, the planet ruled by apes.)
The truck stops fifty yards from us. I pick my son up in my

The last page of the original manuscript of Oscar Wilde's *The Picture of Dorian Gray*. *(The Pierpont Morgan Library, New York, MA 833)* arms and leave the launch. Nova follows us after a moment's hesitation. She looks frightened but she will soon get over it.

The driver gets out of the vehicle. He has his back turned to me. He is half concealed by the long grass growing in the space between us. He opens the door for the passenger to alight. I was not mistaken, he is an officer; a senior officer, as I now see from his badges of rank. He jumps down. He takes a few steps toward us, emerges from the grass, and at last appears in full view. Nova utters a scream, snatches my son from me, and rushes back with him to the launch, while I remain rooted to the spot, unable to move a muscle or utter a sound.

He is a gorilla.

—PIERRE BOULLÉ, *Planet of the Apes,* trans. Xan Fielding

(Sixty years before, as her pursued lover was about to leave her for the Cause, Lady L. had hidden him in the Madras strongbox in her private retreat.)

"Sometimes I cannot bear it," she said. "I just can't bear the idea that one day I will die and lose you forever. I just can't imagine not coming here to be with you, to sit with you, to talk to you, to live with you as I have done almost every day during the last sixty years."

The Poet Laureate finally managed to speak. But his voice came out strangely high and almost eunuchlike, and even then he couldn't find the words.

"You mean to say that he's still—that you have . . . "

Then his voice failed him again and he just sat there, pointing a shaking finger at the thing.

Lady L. took from her pocket a heavy black key and put it into the lock. She turned it twice and opened the door.

Armand was kneeling there in his gray courtier coat. The white knee breeches and the silk stockings adhered to the bones, or hung limply around them. There was a leather bag—with a black mantilla over it. A pistol lay between the buckled shoes. The right hand of the skeleton held a red tulle rose.

—ROMAIN GARY, *Lady L.*

My God, that bloody casket has fallen on the floor! Some people were hammering in the next flat and it fell off its bracket. The lid has come off and whatever was inside it has certainly got out. Upon the demon-ridden pilgrimage of human life, what next I wonder?

—IRIS MURDOCH, *The Sea, The Sea*

"Goodbye, Yossarian," the chaplain called. "And good luck. I'll stay here and persevere, and we'll meet again when the fighting stops."

"So long, Chaplain. Thanks, Danby."

"How do you feel, Yossarian?"

"Fine. No, I'm very frightened."

"That's good," said Major Danby. "It proves you're still alive. It won't be fun."

Yossarian started out. "Yes it will."

"I mean it, Yossarian. You'll have to keep on your toes

every minute of every day. They'll bend heaven and earth to catch you."

"I'll keep on my toes every minute."

"You'll have to jump."

"I'll jump."

"Jump!" Major Danby cried.

Yossarian jumped. Nately's whore was hiding just outside the door. The knife came down, missing him by inches, and he took off.

—JOSEPH HELLER, *Catch-22*

24 ❧ HERO REDUX

y the time we reach the end of a novel, we ought to have some very strong feelings about its hero and heroine. We might love them or hate them, but we should be involved enough to care what happens to them. In fact, if the main character has really lived for us, we may be extremely reluctant to let go of him, and read with increasing regret as the end of the book approaches.

If we as readers feel such empathy for a character, imagine what a novelist faces when he must say good-bye to a creation with whom he has awakened, eaten, slept, drunk, laughed, cried, and dreamed for months or even years. When the character is based entirely or even partially on an actual person, which is often the case, ending the book may mean ending a remembered or imagined relationship with that person, as the author relives the encounter as it happened or rewrites it the way he or she wishes it had happened. But even if the character has come solely from the novelist's imagination, the parting is bittersweet.

So the novelist, bidding good-bye to a hero, may give us one last look, one final image to hold in our memory like a beloved face at the window of a departing train. If it is successful, this last image of the hero or heroine will stay with us long after we close the book. Here is how Kathleen Winsor said good-bye to the heroine of *Forever Amber*: "Amber had picked up her skirts and started to run. Outdoors it was growing light and the sun streaked over the tops of the brick buildings. Her coach stood waiting. As he saw her coming the footman flung open the door and reared back in rigid attention; she laughed and gave a snip of her fingers at his braid-covered chest as she climbed in. Imperturbably he slammed the door, motioned to the driver and the coach rolled forward. Still laughing, she leaned out, and waved at the closed empty windows."

Goodnight, Sweet Princess 🦚
The author bids his creation good-bye.

(Marlow completes his telling of the story of Lord Jim.)
"But we can see him, an obscure conqueror of fame, tearing himself out of the arms of a jealous love at the sign, at the call of his exalted egoism. He goes away from a living woman to celebrate his pitiless wedding with a shadowy ideal of conduct. Is he satisfied—quite, now, I wonder? We ought to know. He is one of us—and have I not stood up once, like

an evoked ghost, to answer for his eternal constancy? Was I
so very wrong after all? Now he is no more, there are days
when the reality of his existence comes to me with an
immense, with an overwhelming force; and yet upon my
honour there are moments, too, when he passes from my
eyes like a disembodied spirit astray amongst the passions of
this earth, ready to surrender himself faithfully to the claim
of his own world of shades.

"Who knows? He is gone, inscrutable at heart, and the
poor girl is leading a sort of soundless, inert life in Stein's
house. Stein has aged greatly of late. He feels it himself,
and says often that he is 'preparing to leave all this; preparing to leave . . .' while he waves his hand sadly at his but-
terflies."

—JOSEPH CONRAD, *Lord Jim*

So said Hester Prynne, and glanced her sad eyes downward
at the scarlet letter. And, after many, many years, a new grave
was delved, near an old and sunken one, in that burial-
ground beside which King's Chapel has since been built. It
was near that old and sunken grave, yet with a space
between, as if the dust of the two sleepers had no right to
mingle. Yet one tombstone served for both. All around, there
were monuments carved with armorial bearings; and on this
simple slab of slate—as the curious investigator may still dis-
cern, and perplex himself with the purport—there appeared
the semblance of an engraved escutcheon. It bore a device, a
herald's wording of which might serve for a motto and brief
description of our now concluded legend; so sombre is it,

and relieved only by one everglowing point of light gloomier than the shadow:—

"ON A FIELD, SABLE, THE LETTER A, GULES."

—NATHANIEL HAWTHORNE, *The Scarlet Letter*

(Temple Drake, rescued from a Memphis brothel, her mind unstable, is taken by her father to live in Paris.)
In the pavilion a band in the horizon blue of the army played Massenet and Scriabine, and Berlioz like a thin coating of tortured Tschaikovsky on a slice of stale bread, while the twilight dissolved in wet gleams from the branches, onto the pavilion and the sombre toadstools of umbrellas. Rich and resonant the brasses crashed and died in the thick green twilight, rolling over them in rich sad waves. Temple yawned behind her hand, then she took out a compact and opened it upon a face in miniature sullen and discontented and sad. Beside her her father sat, his hands crossed on the head of his stick, the rigid bar of his moustache beaded with moisture like frosted silver. She closed the compact and from beneath her smart new hat she seemed to follow with her eyes the waves of music, to dissolve into the dying brasses, across the pool and the opposite semicircle of trees where at sombre intervals the dead tranquil queens in stained marble mused, and on into the sky lying prone and vanquished in the embrace of the season of rain and death.

—WILLIAM FAULKNER, *Sanctuary*

Detail of the last page of the original manuscript of William Faulkner's *Sanctuary*. (*William Faulkner Collections [#6074], Manuscripts Division, Special Collections Department, University of Virginia Library*)

(Humbert Humbert has murdered Clare Quilty for running off with his child lover, Lolita, who marries Richard F. Schiller, and dies in childbirth.)

. . . I wish this memoir to be published only when Lolita is no longer alive.

Thus, neither of us is alive when the reader opens this book. But while the blood still throbs through my writing hand, you are still as much part of blessed matter as I am, and I can still talk to you from here to Alaska. Be true to your Dick. Do not let other fellows touch you. Do not talk to strangers. I hope you will love your baby. I hope it will be a boy. That husband of yours, I hope, will always treat you well, because otherwise my specter shall come at him, like black smoke, like a demented giant, and pull him apart nerve by nerve. And do not pity C.Q. One had to choose between him and H. H., and one wanted H. H. to exist at least a couple of months longer, so as to have him make you live in the minds of later generations. I am thinking of aurochs and angels, the secret of durable pigments, prophetic sonnets, the refuge of art. And this is the only immortality you and I may share, my Lolita.

—VLADIMIR NABOKOV, *Lolita*

This was the road over which Ántonia and I came on that night when we got off the train at Black Hawk and were bedded down in the straw, wondering children, being taken we knew not whither. I had only to close my eyes to hear the rumbling of the wagons in the dark, and to be again overcome by that obliterating strangeness. The feelings of that night were so near that I could reach out and touch them with my hand. I had the sense of coming home to myself, and of having found out what a little circle man's experience is. For Ántonia and for me, this had been the road of Destiny; had taken us to those early accidents of fortune which predetermined for us all that we can ever be. Now I understood that the same road was to bring us together again. Whatever we had missed, we possessed together the precious, the incommunicable past.

—WILLA CATHER, *My Ántonia*

Of Silver we have heard no more. That formidable seafaring man with one leg has at last gone clean out of my life; but I dare say he met his old Negress, and perhaps still lives in comfort with her and Captain Flint. It is to be hoped so, I suppose, for his chances for comfort in another world are very small.

The bar silver and the arms still lie, for all that I know, where Flint buried them; and certainly they shall lie there for me. Oxen and wain-ropes would not bring me back again to that accursed island; and the worst dreams that ever I have are when I hear the surf booming about its coasts, or start upright in bed, with the sharp voice of Captain Flint still ringing in my ears: "Pieces of eight! pieces of eight!"

—ROBERT LOUIS STEVENSON, *Treasure Island*

(Bertie Wooster is determined to fire his valet, Jeeves, for saving the day for a friend of Bertie's by intimating that his employer was "a looney.")

And then through the doorway there shimmered good old Jeeves in the wake of a tray full of the necessary ingredients, and there was something about the mere look of the man. . . .

However, I steeled the old heart and had a stab at it.

"I have just met Mr. Little, Jeeves," I said.

"Indeed, sir?"

"He—er—he told me you had been helping him."

"I did my best, sir. And I am happy to say that matters now appear to be proceeding smoothly. Whisky, sir?"

"Thanks. Er—Jeeves."

"Sir?"

"Another time . . ."

"Sir?"

"Oh, nothing . . . Not all the soda, Jeeves."

"Very good, sir."

He started to drift out.

"Oh, Jeeves!"

"Sir?"

"I wish . . . that is . . . I think . . . I mean . . . Oh, nothing!"

"Very good, sir. The cigarettes are at your elbow, sir. Dinner will be ready at a quarter to eight precisely, unless you desire to dine out?"

"No. I'll dine in."

"Yes, sir."

"Jeeves!"

"Sir?"

"Oh nothing!" I said.

"Very good, sir," said Jeeves.

—P. G. WODEHOUSE, *Jeeves*

25 ❦ THE MASTER THEME

Moving insistently beneath the surface of the plot like a tracer line on an oscilloscope, is the theme, the single idea the author wishes to convey. The plot, the series of events that move the story along, may dance wildly up or down, but here and there it touches the theme line, and each time it does it reminds us what the book is really about.

Often the theme is represented by a symbol, like the land in Pearl Buck's *The Good Earth*, or the tree in Betty Smith's *A Tree Grows in Brooklyn*, or the birds in Colleen McCullough's *The Thorn Birds*, and the author will choose to end the book with the strength of that symbol. And so, aged Wang Lung clenches a handful of soil as his sons lie to him, promising they will never sell the land that he has struggled all his life to own. The tree, chopped down until it is only a stump, finds light amid the wash lines in the Brooklyn backyard and begins to grow again. And Meggie, alone and abandoned forever by her priest-lover, realizes she is like the bird that impales itself on a thorn, yet continues to sing until it dies.

The danger of using symbolism is that the novel runs the risk of becoming a treatise instead of a story if the symbolism is overdone. But used well, it crystallizes the theme, melding all the divergent episodes of the book together into a whole. It gives the story a transcendent meaning.

Variation on a Theme 🍂
The central idea of the book is reprised at the end.

A new tree had grown from the stump and its trunk had grown along the ground until it reached a place where there were no wash lines above it. Then it had started to grow towards the sky again.

Annie, the fir tree, that the Nolans had cherished with waterings and manurings, had long since sickened and died. But this tree in the yard—this tree that men chopped down ... this tree that they built a bonfire around, trying to burn up its stump—this tree lived!

It lived! And nothing could destroy it.

Once more she looked at Florry Wendy reading on the fire escape.

"Goodbye, Francie," she whispered.

She closed the window.

—BETTY SMITH, *A Tree Grows in Brooklyn*

He found himself listening for something. It was the sound of the yearling for which he listened, running around the house or stirring on his moss pallet in the corner of the bedroom. He would never hear him again. He wondered if his mother had thrown dirt over Flag's carcass, or if the buzzards had cleaned it. Flag— He did not believe he should ever again love anything, man or woman or his own child, as he had loved the yearling. He would be lonely all his life. But a man took it for his share and went on.

In the beginning of his sleep, he cried out, "Flag!"

It was not his own voice that called. It was a boy's voice. Somewhere beyond the sink-hole, past the magnolia, under the live oaks, a boy and a yearling ran side by side, and were gone forever.

—MARJORIE KINNAN RAWLINGS, *The Yearling*

"She'll be all right, dear. Look at her! Jove!"

There stood Magnolia Ravenal on the upper deck of the Cotton Blossom Floating Palace Theatre, silhouetted against sunset sky and water—tall, erect, indomitable. Her mouth was smiling but her great eyes were wide and sombre. They gazed, unwinking, across the sunlit waters. One arm was raised in a gesture of farewell.

"Isn't she splendid, Ken!" cried Kim, through her tears. "There's something about her that's eternal and unconquerable—like the River."

A bend in the upper road. A clump of sycamores. The river, the show boat, the straight silent figure were lost to view.

—EDNA FERBER, *Show Boat*

(Meggie Cleary muses on the cycle of Nature and her life, from the window of her home, the Australian sheep station, Drogheda.)
Time for Drogheda to stop. Yes, more than time. Let the cycle renew itself with unknown people. I did it all to myself, I have no one else to blame. And I cannot regret one single moment of it.

The bird with the thorn in its breast, it follows an immutable law; it is driven by it knows not what to impale itself, and die singing. At the very instant the thorn enters there is no awareness in it of the dying to come; it simply sings and sings until there is not the life left to utter another note. But we, when we put the thorns in our breasts, we know. We understand. And still we do it. Still we do it.

—COLLEEN MCCULLOUGH, *The Thorn Birds*

(The scheming Becky Sharp, widowed, wealthy, and calling herself Lady Crawley, busies herself with good works and is considered "an injured woman.")
. . . Her name is in all the Charity Lists. The Destitute Orange-girl, the Neglected Washerwoman, the Distressed Muffin-man, find in her a fast and generous friend. She is always having stalls at Fancy Fairs for the benefit of these hapless beings. Emmy, her children, and the Colonel, coming to London some time back, found themselves suddenly before her at one of these fairs. She cast down her eyes demurely and smiled as they started away from her; Emmy skurrying off on the arm of George (now grown a dashing young gentleman), and the Colonel seizing up his little Janey,

of whom he is fonder than of anything in the world—fonder even than of his "History of the Punjaub."

"Fonder than he is of me," Emmy thinks, with a sigh. But he never said a word to Amelia that was not kind and gentle; or thought of a want of hers that he did not try to gratify.

Ah! *Vanitas Vanitatum!* which of us is happy in this world? Which of us has his desire? or, having it, is satisfied?—come, children, let us shut up the box and the puppets, for our play is played out.

—WILLIAM MAKEPEACE THACKERAY, *Vanity Fair*

And the old man let his scanty tears dry upon his cheeks and they made salty stains there. And he stooped and took up a handful of the soil and he held it and he muttered,

"If you sell the land, it is the end."

And his two sons held him, one on either side, each holding his arm, and he held tight in his hand the warm loose earth. And they soothed him and they said over and over, the elder son and the second son,

"Rest assured, our father, rest assured. The land is not to be sold."

But over the old man's head they looked at each other and smiled.

—PEARL BUCK, *The Good Earth*

26 ❦ ONCE UPON A TITLE

ew things are more mysterious or fascinating than the creative process. Where does an idea come from? How does it develop along the lines it does? Why does the author make the choices he or she makes? In the business world, "facilitators" lead brainstorming sessions that attempt to imitate the way the creative mind works. Significantly, although they begin with a stated objective, for example, to find a name for a new product, their method is not to focus on that problem, but to encourage the mind to roam freely. Thus they might ask participants for words to describe the sea, in the case of a shaving lotion, or a barbecue, in the case of a new fast food, and then cull from those free associations combinations of words that suggest themselves as names. The success of these sessions in broadening thinking was considered innovative, but the process is the same the creative mind uses subconsciously. It is taking the mind by surprise.

The process can easily be observed in the author's choice of a title.

Sometimes the title will be the first thing that comes to the writer, even before a word has been written. But just as often it will be the last, changing and evolving throughout the writing itself, and appearing as an entry on a list of lesser possibilities. Thus *Lady Chatterley's Lover* began as *My Lady's Keeper; The Age of Innocence* as *Old New York; The Sun Also Rises* variously as *Fiesta, The Last Generation, River to the Sea, Two Lie Together,* and *The Old Leaven;* and *Gone with the Wind* as *The Road to Tara, Another Day, Tomorrow Is Another Day, Tomorrow and Tomorrow, There's Always Tomorrow,* and *Tomorrow Will Be Fair.*

The mind free-associates, but there is a single objective: the title must epitomize the author's theme. It must indicate, to the author at least, what the book is about. Thus we have illustrative titles like *Rabbit Is Rich, Brideshead Revisited, Catch-22, Pride and Prejudice, Vanity Fair,* and *Under the Volcano.* Sometimes the meaning of the title is clear to the reader from the beginning of the book. But often this revelation is saved for the last page, even the last sentence. There it has the effect of bringing the book full circle. We began with the title, wondering what it meant, and we end with the title, its meaning now clear to us.

The Name of the Game 🦋
The novel ends with the title.

He fell in October, 1918, on a day that was so quiet and still on the whole front, that the army report confined itself to the single sentence: All quiet on the Western Front.

He had fallen forward and lay on the earth as though sleeping. Turning him over one saw that he could not have suffered long; his face had an expression of calm, as though almost glad the end had come.

—ERICH MARIA REMARQUE,
All Quiet on the Western Front,
trans. A. W. Wheen

(Linford, a new boy, has visited the beloved master, Chips, at Brookfield School before his death.)
And soon Chips was asleep.

He seemed so peaceful that they did not disturb him to say good-night; but in the morning, as the School bell sounded for breakfast, Brookfield had the news. "Brookfield will never forget his lovableness," said Cartwright, in a speech to the School. Which was absurd, because all things are forgotten in the end. But Linford, at any rate, will remember and tell the tale: "I said good-bye to Chips the night before he died. . . ."

—JAMES HILTON, *Good-bye, Mr. Chips*

(Sandy, who as a schoolgirl had informed on her eccentric teacher, Miss Brodie, has become Sister Helena of the Transfiguration.)
Monica came again. "Before she died," she said, "Miss Brodie thought it was you who betrayed her."

"It's only possible to betray where loyalty is due," said Sandy.

"Well, wasn't it due to Miss Brodie?"

"Only up to a point," said Sandy.

And there was that day when the enquiring young man came to see Sandy because of her strange book of psychology, "The Transfiguration of the Commonplace," which had brought so many visitors that Sandy clutched the bars of her grille more desperately than ever.

"What were the main influences of your school days, Sister Helena? Were they literary or political or personal? Was it Calvinism?"

Sandy said: "There was a Miss Jean Brodie in her prime."

—MURIEL SPARK, *The Prime of Miss Jean Brodie*

Chingachgook grasped the hand that, in the warmth of feeling, the scout had stretched across the fresh earth, and in that attitude of friendship these two sturdy and intrepid woodsmen bowed their heads together, while scalding tears fell to their feet, watering the grave of Uncas like drops of falling rain.

In the midst of the awful stillness with which such a burst of feeling, coming, as it did, from the two most renowned warriors of that region, was received, Tamenund lifted his voice to disperse the multitude.

"It is enough," he said. "Go, children of the Lenape, the anger of the Manitou is not done. Why should Tamenund stay? The pale-faces are masters of the earth, and the time of the redmen has not yet come again. My day has been too long. In the morning I saw the sons of Unamis happy and strong; and yet, before the night has come, have I lived to see the last warrior of the wise race of the Mohicans."

—JAMES FENIMORE COOPER, *The Last of the Mohicans*

. . . From all across the hot distances of the plain there was no breath of sound. In the small bare room with its bamboo-shaded windows there was no glitter of sun. He picked up the stem of the frangipani flower and held it in his hands. The flowers were still blooming, as the girl had said they would be, with rosy half-opened buds of blossom, and he remembered now that they stood for immortality.

Breathing in the scent of them in a great gasp that was like an agony of relief and pleasure, he lay with his body against her and shut his eyes. Her body felt young and trembling with the breath of sleep and now there was nothing more he asked for but to lie beside it and sleep too.

Outside, the plain was purple in the falling dusk, and the long day was over.

—H. E. BATES, *The Purple Plain*

Maule's well, all this time, though left in solitude, was throwing up a succession of kaleidoscopic pictures, in which a gifted eye might have seen foreshadowed the coming fortunes of Hepzibah and Clifford, and the descendant of the legendary wizard, and the village maiden, over whom he had thrown Love's web of sorcery. The Pyncheon Elm, moreover, with what foliage the September gale had spared to it, whispered unintelligible prophecies. And wise Uncle Venner, passing slowly from the ruinous porch, seemed to hear a strain of music, and fancied that sweet Alice Pyncheon—after witnessing these deeds, this bygone woe and this present happiness, of her kindred mortals— had given one farewell touch of a spirit's joy upon her harpsichord, as she floated heavenward from the HOUSE OF THE SEVEN GABLES!

—NATHANIEL HAWTHORNE, *The House of the Seven Gables*

(Huw Morgan remembers his Welsh home and the minister who inspired him to leave it.)
Is Mr. Gruffydd dead, him, that one of rock and flame, who was friend and mentor, who gave me his watch that was all in the world he had, because he loved me? Is he dead, and the tears still wet on my face and my voice cutting through rocks in my throats for minutes while I tried to say good-bye, and, O God, the words were shy to come, and I went from him wordless, in tears and with blood.

Is he dead?

For if he is, then I am dead, and we are dead, and all of sense a mockery.

How green was my Valley, then, and the Valley of them that have gone.

—RICHARD LLEWELLYN, *How Green Was My Valley*

"One thing more," said George, as he stopped the congratulations of the throng; "you all remember our good old Uncle Tom?"

George here gave a short narration of the scene of his death, and of his loving farewell to all on the place, and added,

"It was on his grave, my friends, that I resolved, before God, that I would never own another slave, while it was possible to free him; that nobody, through me, should ever run the risk of being parted from home and friends, and dying on a lonely plantation, as he died. So, when you rejoice in your freedom, think that you owe it to that good old soul, and pay it back in kindness to his wife and children. Think of your freedom, every time you see UNCLE TOM'S CABIN; and let it be a memorial to put you all in mind to follow in his steps, and be as honest and faithful and Christian as he was."

—HARRIET BEECHER STOWE, *Uncle Tom's Cabin*

27 ❧ SHEER POETRY

t was a popular practice in the early years of the novel to begin each chapter with a line or verse of poetry that indicated the tenor of the chapter that was to follow. Poetry or scriptural quotations were also popularly used to *end* books, elevating the text to a plane that was necessarily more ethereal than pure prose. Poetry added a symbolic, often ironic, emphasis to a novel's conclusion. Sometimes the verse came like a benediction.

Although beginning chapters with verse is less popular today, ending with verse can hardly be considered outdated when it has been used by contemporary authors as varied as Paul Scott, Thomas Pynchon, Günter Grass, and Leon Uris. If the author is also a poet, the verse that ends the book might even be original. Otherwise it could be a bit of doggerel, a biblical quotation, a nursery rhyme, a song, or a fragment of a prayer.

A Turn for the Verse 🌿
Poetry says it all.

Ivanhoe distinguished himself in the service of Richard, and was graced with farther marks of the royal favour. He might have risen still higher, but for the premature death of the heroic Coeur-de-Lion, before the Castle of Chaluz, near Limoges. With the life of a generous, but rash and romantic monarch, perished all the projects which his ambition and his generosity had formed; to whom may be applied, with a slight alteration, the lines composed by Johnson for Charles of Sweden—

> His fate was destined to a foreign strand,
> A petty fortress and an "humble" hand;
> He left the name at which the world grew pale,
> To point a moral, or adorn a TALE.
> —SIR WALTER SCOTT, *Ivanhoe*

(In a deserted corner of the potter's field of the cemetery of Père Lachaise in Paris is the grave of Jean Valjean.)
. . . This stone is exempt no more than the rest from the leprosy of time, from the mould, the lichen, and the droppings of the birds. The air turns it black, the water green. It is near no path, and people do not like to go in that direction, because the grass is high, and they would wet their feet. When there is a little sunshine, the lizards come out. There is, all about, a

rustling of wild oats. In the spring, the linnets sing in the tree.

This stone is entirely blank. The only thought in cutting it was of the essentials of the grave, and there was no other care than to make this stone long enough and narrow enough to cover a man.

No name can be read there.

Only many years ago, a hand wrote upon it in pencil these four lines which have become gradually illegible under the rain and the dust, and which are probably effaced:

Il dort. Quoique le sort fût pour lui bien étrange,
Il vivait. Il mourut quand il n'eut plus son ange.
La chose simplement d'elle-même arriva,
Comme la nuit se fait lorsque le jour s'en va. *

—VICTOR HUGO, *Les Misérables*,
trans. Charles E. Wilbour

(After Billy Budd's death, a ballad, "Billy in the Darbies," is circulated among the crew.)

. . . Ay, Ay, all is up; and I must up too
Early in the morning, aloft from alow.

---

* *He sleeps. He lived though fate to him was strange,*
His angel left him and he died; the change
Came in a natural and simple way,
As night is made when fades from sight the day.

(trans. M. Jules Gray)

On an empty stomach, now, never it would do.
They'll give me a nibble—bit o' biscuit ere I go.
Sure, a messmate will reach me the last parting cup;
But, turning heads away from the hoist and the belay,
Heaven knows who will have the running of me up!
No pipe to those halyards.—But aren't it all sham?
A blur's in my eyes; it is dreaming that I am.
A hatchet to my hawser? all adrift to go?
The drum roll to grog, and Billy never know?
But Donald he has promised to stand by the plank;
So I'll shake a friendly hand ere I sink.
But—no! It is dead then I'll be, come to think.—
I remember Taff the Welshman when he sank.
And his cheek it was like the budding pink.
But me they'll lash me in hammock, drop me deep.
Fathoms down, fathoms down, how I'll dream fast asleep.
I feel it stealing now. Sentry, are you there?
Just ease this darbies at the wrist, and roll me over fair,
I am sleepy, and the oozy weeds about me twist.

—HERMAN MELVILLE, *Billy Budd*

(Guy Perron reflects as the English leave India to independence and partition, remembering an Indian poem he now knows by heart.)

Everything means something to you; dying flowers,
The different times of year.
The new clothes you wear at the end of Ramadan.
A prince's trust. The way that water flows,
Too impetuous to pause, breaking over

Stones, rushing towards distant objects,
Places you can't see but which you also flow
Outward to.

Today you slept long. When you woke your old blood
stirred.
This too meant something. The girl who woke you
Touched your brow.
She called you Lord. You smiled,
Put up a trembling hand. But she had gone,
As seasons go, as a night-flower closes in the day,
As a hawk flies into the sun or as the cheetah runs; as
The deer pauses, sun-dappled in long grass,
But does not stay.

Fleeting moments: these are held a long time in the eye,
The blind eye of the ageing poet,
So that even you, Gaffur, can imagine
In this darkening landscape
The bowman lovingly choosing his arrow,
The hawk outpacing the cheetah,
(The fountain splashing lazily in the courtyard),
The girl running with the deer.

—PAUL SCOTT, *The Raj Quartet [A Division of the Spoils]*

She is silent, she will never speak, never forgive, never reach
a hand, never leave this frozen present tense. All waits, sus-

pended. Suspend the autumn trees, the autumn sky, anonymous people. A blackbird, poor fool, sings out of season from the willows by the lake. A flight of pigeons over the houses; fragments of freedom, hazard, an anagram made flesh. And somewhere the stinging smell of burning leaves.

> *cras amet qui numquam amavit*
> *quique amavit cras amet**
>
> —JOHN FOWLES, *The Magus*

* Tomorrow let him love who never
    loved before
Whoever has loved and loves no longer,
    let him love tomorrow.

(trans. John Leich)

28 ❦ THE EPILOGUE

What the prologue is to the beginning of the book, the epilogue is to the end. It can leap years ahead to show how life progressed for the novel's characters as we last saw them, just as the prologue stepped back to give us some of their history before we met them in the first chapter. It can wax philosophic or provide information to illuminate what we have just read. It can permit the author or faux-author (the novelist masquerading as the "writer" of the book) to express personal feelings about the story just told. It can take the form of an appendix, providing the verbatim report of an inquest, a newspaper story or a personal letter to cast light on an otherwise inconclusive ending. And it can bring a story told as a flashback back into the present.

Like the prologue, the epilogue—or conclusion, or finale, as it is variously called—gives the author the option of having a second ending. Thus the novelist can end the story on a high pitch with some action: a marriage, a rescue or a death, for instance, then conclude with a more introspective chapter. The epilogue frees the author from the confines of the story.

In his novel *The French Lieutenant's Woman*, John Fowles even used the last chapter, which is not called an epilogue but functions as one, to rewrite his happy ending with an unhappy one. Fowles introduced a new character, an "impresario," representing Time or Fowles himself as creator, to turn the clock back a quarter of an hour, so that we might read a different ending from the same moment in time. What is interesting is that both endings are completely plausible, and therefore, acceptable to us, even though our emotions are a bit ragged because of the trick that has been played on us. Was the duplicate ending more than a conscious betrayal of the reader? Did Fowles, himself unable to decide between two equally dramatic and intriguing endings, choose to have them both? Which ending did he prefer? Did he rebel against sentencing his romantically mysterious heroine to the conventional marriage that would have been required by the conventionally "happy" ending? In the last analysis, there is some hope even in the second, "unhappy" version, for as Charles Smithson grieves at the loss of Sarah Woodruff to the household of the Rossettis and life as a "New Woman," he has at least found "an atom of faith in himself" on which to build his life again "upon the unplumb'd, salt, estranging sea."

For Tolstoy, finishing *War and Peace*, a single epilogue was not enough (how could it be?), and so he wrote two: the first, which in typical epilogue style picks up the story eight years after the death of Prince Andrey, recounting the happy domestic lives of Pierre and Natasha and Princess Mary and Nicholas after their marriages; and the second, which expounds on the historian's study of human life, free will and necessity, and the forces behind national movements. Most epilogues are not as intricately conceived as this one, which compares in length and complexity to a Shavian preface, but are simply dramatic codas to the stories that have gone before. As they shed further light on a character or an outcome, they are welcome additions to the story and a vital part of the novel itself.

How Tempus Fugits! 🎉
The epilogue spans the years.

(Roger Byam returns to Tahiti eighteen years after he has been taken back to England and finally acquitted of mutiny, to find that his wife, Tehani, has died and his daughter, also called Tehani, has a child.)
"Tehani," called the man beside me, and I caught my breath as she turned, for she had all her dead mother's beauty, and something of my own mother, as well. "The English captain from Matavai," Tuahu was saying, and she gave me her hand graciously. My granddaughter was staring up at me in wonder, and I turned away blindly.

"We must go on," said Tehani to her uncle. "I promised the child she should see the English boat."

"Aye, go," replied Tuahu.

The moon was bright overhead when I reëmbarked in the pinnace to return to my ship. A chill night breeze came whispering down from the depths of the valley, and suddenly the place was full of ghosts,—shadows of men alive and dead,—my own among them.

—CHARLES NORDHOFF AND JAMES NORMAN HALL, Epilogue, *Mutiny on the Bounty*

(His street evangelist mother carries on her life and mission after the execution of her son, Clyde, for murder.)

"Kin' I have a dime, grandma? I wana' go up to the corner and git an ice-cream cone." It was the boy asking.

"Yes, I guess so, Russell. But listen to me. You are to come right back."

"Yes, I will, grandma, sure. You know me."

He took the dime that his Grandmother had extracted from a deep pocket in her dress and ran with it to the ice-cream vendor.

Her darling boy. The light and color of her declining years. She must be kind to him, more liberal with him, not restrain him too much, as maybe, maybe, she had—— She looked affectionately and yet a little vacantly after him as he ran. "For *his* sake."

The small company, minus Russell, entered the yellow, unprepossessing door and disappeared.

—THEODORE DREISER, Souvenir, *An American Tragedy*

(D'Artagnan has taken the commission refused by the musketeers: Porthos, who has left the service to marry a rich widow; Aramis, who has retired to a convent; and Athos, who has retired after inheriting a small property. And the cardinal's informant, the husband of the Queen's faithful servant whom the musketeers had rescued . . .) M. Bonacieux lived on very quietly, wholly ignorant of what had become of his wife, and caring very little about it. One day he had the imprudence to recall himself to the memory of the cardinal. The cardinal had him informed that he would provide for him so that he should never want for anything in future. In fact, M. Bonacieux, having left his house at seven o'clock in the evening to go to the Louvre, never appeared again in the Rue des Fossoyeurs; the opinion of those who seemed to be best informed was that he was fed and lodged in some royal castle, at the expense of his generous Eminence.

—ALEXANDRE DUMAS, Epilogue, *The Three Musketeers*

(Seven years after the death of his father, Prince Andrey comes to his son Nikolinka in a dream, and the boy awakes in terror.) "My father!" he thought. (Although there were two very good portraits of Prince Andrey in the house, Nikolinka never thought of his father in human form.) "My father has been with me, and has caressed me. He approved of me; he approved of Uncle Pierre. Whatever he might tell me, I would do it. Mucius Scaevola burnt his hand. But why should not the same sort of thing happen in my life? I know they want me to study. And I am going to study. But some

day I shall have finished, and then I will act. One thing only I pray God for, that the same sort of thing may happen with me as with Plutarch's men, and I will act in the same way. I will do more. Every one shall know of me, shall love me, and admire me." And all at once Nikolinka felt his breast heaving with sobs, and he burst into tears.

"Are you ill?" he heard Dessalle's voice.

"No," answered Nikolinka, and he lay back on his pillow. "How good and kind he is; I love him!" He thought of Dessalle. "But Uncle Pierre! Oh, what a wonderful man! And my father? Father! Father! Yes, I will do something that even *he* would be content with . . ."

—COUNT LEO TOLSTOY, First Epilogue, *War and Peace*, trans. Constance Garnett

(Karamazov's youngest son, Alyosha, speaks at the funeral of a schoolboy friend as he prepares to accompany his brother Dmitri, wrongly accused of their father's death, to Siberia.)

"Karamazov," cried Kolya, "can it be true what's taught us in religion, that we shall all rise again from the dead and shall live and see each other again, all, Ilusha too?"

"Certainly we shall all rise again, certainly we shall see each other and shall tell each other with joy and gladness all that has happened!" Alyosha answered, half laughing, half enthusiastic.

"Ah, how splendid it will be!" broke from Kolya.

"Well, now we will finish talking and go to his funeral dinner. Don't be put out at our eating pancakes—it's a very old custom and there's something nice in that!" laughed Alyosha. "Well, let us go! And now we go hand in hand."

"And always so, all our lives hand in hand! Hurrah for Karamazov!" Kolya cried once more rapturously, and once more the boys took up his exclamation:

"Hurrah for Karamazov!"

—FYODOR DOSTOYEVSKY,
Epilogue, *The Brothers Karamazov*,
trans. Constance Garnett

The Epilogue as Appendix 🎋
Some further information makes it all clear.

(The keeper of the inn called The Invisible Man gloats over the secret manuscripts left by that strange creature.)
His brows are knit and his lips move painfully. "Hex, little two up in the air, cross and a fiddle-de-dee. Lord! what a one he was for intellect!"

Presently he relaxes and leans back, and blinks through his smoke across the room at things invisible to other eyes. "Full of secrets," he says. Wonderful secrets!

"Once I get the haul of them—*Lord!*

"I wouldn't do what *he* did; I'd just—well!" He pulls at his pipe.

So he lapses into a dream, the undying wonderful dream of his life. And though Kemp has fished unceasingly, and Adye has questioned closely, no human being save the land-lord knows those books are there, with the subtle secret of invisibility and a dozen other strange secrets written therein. And none other will know of them until he dies.

　　　　　　　—H. G. WELLS, The Epilogue, *The Invisible Man*

. . . Half an hour from now, when I shall again and forever reindue that hated personality, I know how I shall sit shuddering and weeping in my chair, or continue, with the most strained and fearstruck ecstasy of listening, to pace up and down this room (my last earthly refuge) and give ear to every sound of menace. Will Hyde die upon the scaffold? or will he find courage to release himself at the last moment? God knows; I am careless; this is my true hour of death, and what is to follow concerns another than myself. Here then, as I lay down the pen and proceed to seal up my confession, I bring the life of that unhappy Henry Jekyll to an end.

　　　　　　　—ROBERT LOUIS STEVENSON,
　　　　　　　Henry Jekyll's Full Statement of the Case,
　　　　　　　The Strange Case of Dr. Jekyll and Mr. Hyde

When we got home we were talking of the old time—which we could all look back on without despair, for Godalming and Seward are both happily married. I took the papers from the safe where they had been ever since our return so long ago. We were struck with the fact, that in all the mass of material of which the record is composed, there is hardly one authentic document; nothing but a mass of typewriting, except the later note-books of Mina and Seward and myself, and Van Helsing's memorandum. We could hardly ask any one, even did we wish to, to accept these as proofs of so wild a story. Van Helsing summed it all up as he said, with our boy on his knee:—

"We want no proofs; we ask none to believe us! This boy will some day know what a brave and gallant woman his mother is. Already he knows her sweetness and loving care; later on he will understand how some men so loved her, that they did dare much for her sake."

JONATHAN HARKER.

—BRAM STOKER, Note, *Dracula*

I have prayed over his mortal remains, that God might show him mercy notwithstanding his crimes. Yes, I am sure, quite sure that I prayed beside his body, the other day, when they took it from the spot where they were burying the phonographic records. It was his skeleton. I did not recognize it by the ugliness of the head, for all men are ugly when they have been dead as long as that, but by the plain gold ring which he wore and which Christine Daaé had certainly slipped on his finger, when she came to bury him in accordance with her promise.

The skeleton was lying near the little well, in the place where the Angel of Music first held Christine Daaé fainting in his trembling arms, on the night when he carried her down to the cellars of the Opera house.

And, now, what do they mean to do with that skeleton?

Surely they will not bury it in the common grave! . . . I say
that the place of the skeleton of the Opera ghost is in the
archives of the National Academy of Music. It is no ordinary
skeleton.

—GASTON LEROUX, Epilogue, *The Phantom of the Opera*

*(Ishmael, the lone survivor, tells of his escape from the sinking
whaler,* Pequod.*)*
. . . So, floating on the margin of the ensuing scene, and in
full sight of it, when the half-spent suction of the sunk ship
reached me, I was then, but slowly, drawn towards the closing
vortex. When I reached it, it had subsided to a creamy pool.
Round and round, then, and ever contracting towards the
button-like black bubble at the axis of that slowly wheeling
circle, like another Ixion, I did revolve. Till, gaining that vital
centre, the black bubble upward burst; and now, liberated by
the reason of its cunning spring, and owing to its great buoy-
ancy, rising with great force, the coffin life-buoy shot length-
wise from the sea, fell over, and floated by my side. Buoyed
up by that coffin, for almost one whole day and night, I
floated on a soft and dirge-like main. The unharming sharks,
they glided by as if with padlocks on their mouths; the savage
sea-hawks sailed with sheathed beaks. On the second day, a
sail drew near, nearer, and picked me up at last. It was with
the devious-cruising *Rachel*, that in her retracing search after
her missing children, only found another orphan.

—HERMAN MELVILLE, Epilogue, *Moby-Dick*

Flash Forward 🌿

The author or narrator brings us back to the present.

(Charles Ryder revisits the chapel at Brideshead and reasons with himself.)

"Something quite remote from anything the builders intended, has come out of their work, and out of the fierce little human tragedy in which I played; something none of us thought about at the time; a small red flame—a beaten-copper lamp of deplorable design relit before the beaten-copper doors of a tabernacle; the flame which the old knights saw from their tombs, which they saw put out; that flame burns again for other soldiers, far from home, farther, in heart, than Acre or Jerusalem. It could not have been lit but for the builders and the tragedians, and there I found it this morning, burning anew among the old stones."

I quickened my pace and reached the hut which served us for our ante-room.

"You're looking unusually cheerful today," said the second-in-command.

—EVELYN WAUGH, Epilogue, *Brideshead Revisited*

The river of life, of mysterious laws and mysterious choice, flows past a deserted embankment; and along that other deserted embankment Charles now begins to pace, a man behind the invisible gun carriage on which rests his own corpse. He walks towards an imminent, self-given death? I

The last page of the original manuscript of Evelyn Waugh's *Brideshead Revisited. (Harry Ransom Humanities Research Center, The University of Texas at Austin)* think not; for he has at last found an atom of faith in himself, a true uniqueness, on which to build; has already begun, though he would still bitterly deny it, though there are tears in his eyes to support his denial, to realize that life, however advantageously Sarah may in some ways seem to fit the role of Sphinx, is not a symbol, is not one riddle and one failure to guess it, is not to inhabit one face alone or to be given up after one losing throw of the dice; but is to be, however inadequately, emptily, hopelessly into the city's iron heart, endured. And out again, upon the unplumb'd, salt, estranging sea.

—JOHN FOWLES, Epilogue, *The French Lieutenant's Woman*

. . . A new Theresa will hardly have the opportunity of reforming a conventual life, any more than a new Antigone will spend her heroic piety in daring all for the sake of a brother's burial: the medium in which their ardent deeds took shape is for ever gone. But we insignificant people with our daily words and acts are preparing the lives of many Dorotheas, some of which may present a far sadder sacrifice than that of the Dorothea whose story we know.

Her finely-touched spirit had still its fine issues, though they were not widely visible. Her full nature, like that river of which Cyrus broke the strength, spent itself in channels which had no great name on the earth. But the effect of her being on those around her was incalculably diffusive: for the growing good of the world is partly dependent on unhistoric acts; and that things are not so ill with you and me as they might have been, is half owing to the number who lived faithfully a hidden life, and rest in unvisited tombs.

—GEORGE ELIOT, Finale, *Middlemarch*

(After his sentence and imprisonment in Siberia, with a New Testament given him by Sonia, Raskolnikoff experiences a rebirth.)

. . . He had asked her for it himself not long before his illness and she brought him the book without a word. Till now he had not opened it.

He did not open it now, but one thought passed through his mind: "Can her convictions not be mine now? Her feelings, her aspirations at least. . . ."

She too had been greatly agitated that day, and at night she was taken ill again. But she was so happy—and so unexpectedly happy—that she was almost frightened of her happiness. Seven years, *only* seven years! At the beginning of their happiness at some moments they were both ready to look on those seven years as though they were seven days. He did not know that the new life would not be given him for nothing, that he would have to pay dearly for it, that it would cost him great striving, great suffering.

But that is the beginning of a new story—the story of the gradual renewal of a man, the story of his gradual regeneration, of his passing from one world into another, of his initiation into a new unknown life. That might be the subject of a new story, but our present story is ended.

—FYODOR DOSTOYEVSKY,
Epilogue, *Crime and Punishment*,
trans. Constance Garnett

29 ❧ AUTHOR! AUTHOR!

n the beginning of this book, we saw how the author sometimes intruded into the novel, introducing the story as him- or herself or as another, fictional writer, whom we called the faux-author. By this most elemental method of storytelling, the author was able to speak directly to the reader, establishing a feeling of intimacy, and then slowly to withdraw from the story as it took on its own momentum.

Not surprisingly in books where the author has begun as storyteller, the author usually reappears at the end. This allows a certain distancing from the story, so the novelist can comment on it and its characters, express philosophic views, and even contradict what appears to have happened. This last possibility is particularly effective and amusing when the author is pretending to be the discoverer of a journal or other manuscript, and continues the charade by disclaiming personal responsibility for the story.

The reappearance of the author, far from presenting an unsettling intrusion, should renew the pact of confidentiality the author established with the reader at the beginning of the book. The power of this sense of intimacy, of one voice speaking to another, is enormous. It is a phenomenon very unlike the feeling we experience in a theater, where the audience is an active participant and we are one of many. In a book, the author is talking to us alone. It is why we feel that we *know* a writer.

And what could be more remarkable than *knowing* Jane Austen or D. H. Lawrence or Ernest Hemingway!

And Then I Wrote . . . 🦚
The author or faux-author puts down his pen.

("... *if the reader will allow me to seize him affectionately by the arm," writes the author, "we will together take our last farewell of Barset and of the towers of Barchester."*)
... I may not boast that any beside myself have so realized the place, and the people, and the facts, as to make such reminiscences possible as those which I should attempt to evoke by an appeal to perfect fellowship. But to me Barset has been a real county, and its city a real city, and the spires and towers have been before my eyes, and the voices of the people are known to my ears, and the pavements of the city ways are familiar to my footsteps. To them all I now say farewell. That I have been induced to wander among them too long by my love of old friendships, and by the sweetness of old faces, is a fault for which I may perhaps be more read-

ily forgiven, when I repeat, with some solemnity of assurance, the promise made in my title, that this shall be the last
chronicle of Barset.

—ANTHONY TROLLOPE, *The Last Chronicle of Barset*

As for Davie and Catriona, I shall watch you pretty close in
the next days, and see if you are so bold as to be laughing at
papa and mamma. It is true we were not so wise as we might
have been, and made a great deal of sorrow out of nothing;
but you will find as you grow up that even the artful Miss
Barbara, and even the valiant Mr. Alan, will be not so very
much wiser than their parents. For the life of man upon this
world of ours is a funny business. They talk of the angels
weeping; but I think they must more often be holding their
sides, as they look on; and there was one thing I determined
to do when I began this long story, and that was to tell out
everything as it befell.

—ROBERT LOUIS STEVENSON, *David Balfour*

But I must stop rambling. I must cease my everlasting specu-
lations. If I am ever to write anything, even if I give it my
whole lifetime, I must still make a beginning. I must still
make a mark on the acres of white paper that seem to unroll
before me like arctic snows. And I must shut with a man's
firmness a journal which seems the softest of self-indulgences
in contrast to the austerely empty notebook that now I open.

—LOUIS AUCHINCLOSS, *The Rector of Justin*

And now, as I close my task, subduing my desire to linger yet, these faces fade away. But one face, shining on me like a Heavenly light by which I see all other objects, is above them and beyond them all. And that remains.

I turn my head, and see it, in its beautiful serenity, beside me. My lamp burns low, and I have written far into the night; but the dear presence, without which I were nothing, bears me company.

Oh Agnes, oh my soul, so may thy face be by me when I close my life indeed; so may I, when realities are melting from me like the shadows which I now dismiss, still find thee near me, pointing upward!

—CHARLES DICKENS,
The Personal History of David Copperfield

. . . That is all I can tell of him: I know it is very unsatisfactory; I can't help it. But as I was finishing this book, uneasily conscious that I must leave my reader in the air and seeing no way to avoid it, I looked back with my mind's eye on my long narrative to see if there was any way in which I could devise a more satisfactory ending; and to my intense surprise it dawned upon me that without in the least intending to I had written nothing more nor less than a success story. For all the persons with whom I have been concerned got what they wanted: Elliott social eminence; Isabel an assured position backed by a substantial fortune in an active and cultured community; Gray a steady and lucrative job, with an office to go to from nine till six every day; Suzanne Rouvier security; Sophie death; and Larry happiness. And however superciliously the highbrows carp, we the public in our heart of hearts all like a success story; so perhaps my ending is not so unsatisfactory after all.

—W. SOMERSET MAUGHAM, *The Razor's Edge*

30 ❦ THE END

ife doesn't end. But novels do, and with them the lives and thoughts and dreams we have shared for so short and magical a time. We leave the characters of a book at the zenith of their lives or in the hours of their deaths, and there they remain for us frozen in time. What a weighty responsibility for the author, then, to produce a great ending, one that may grieve or uplift us, but that may also leave us with an indelible memory of the essence and truth of another human being in another time and place.

Just as the beginnings in this book demonstrated that there is no single right way to begin a book, the endings show there are infinite ways to end it, each one unique to its own characters and story and the style of its author. Which is the most successful? Who is to say? Certainly we all have our favorite last images. The green light at the end of the pier in

The Great Gatsby. The ravaged fish tied to the boat in *The Old Man and the Sea.*

Why do these endings please us? The answer goes deeper than the beauty of the writing and the satisfaction of an inevitable conclusion. In observing the life and sometimes the death of another being, we ourselves understand more about life and death. Even if the death is a senseless one, we can experience it objectively from a distance. And as we read, we feel a little more secure, having been let in on something of the Great Mystery. Unlike our reactions to real-life tragedy—frustration, anger, fear, helplessness, and bewilderment in the face of victimized goodness and unpunished evil—the end of the novel in its completeness and closure gives us a feeling, however brief, of control, of evil vanquished and righteousness restored.

The novelist is a just and reasonable god.

Copyright Acknowledgments ❦

Author Index ❦

Title Index 🦎